LIVE THE LIFE YOU LOVE

Published by
Delacorte Press
Bantam Doubleday Dell Publishing Group, Inc.
1540 Broadway
New York, New York 10036

Copyright © 1996 by Barbara Sher

All rights reserved. No part of this book may be reproduced or
transmitted in any form or by any means, electronic or mechanical,
including photocopying, recording, or by any information storage and
retrieval system, without the written permission of the Publisher,
except where permitted by law.

The trademark Delacorte Press® is registered in the U.S. Patent
and Trademark Office.

Library of Congress Cataloging in Publication Data

Sher, Barbara.
Live the life you love in ten easy step-by-step lessons / by Barbara Sher.
p.   cm.
ISBN 0-385-31662-3 (HC)
1. Self-actualization (Psychology)   2. Goal (Psychology)   I. Title.
BF637.S4S523   1996
158'.1—dc20   95-49225
                                                                   CIP

Manufactured in the United States of America
Published simultaneously in Canada

March 1996

10   9   8   7   6   5   4   3   2   1

BVG

For
my sons Danny and Matthew;
through the years,
always my friends.

I want to thank my brilliant friends and editors with all my heart. They read and re-read these pages and gave me extraordinarily helpful suggestions and insights. Thanks, Phyllis Maddox, Adam Nadler, Matthew Pearl, and Judith Riven.

Many thanks to Cyndi and Rich West whose idea it was that I create this program, who nagged and cajoled until it was finished, and who worked tirelessly to turn it into the audiotape series that led to this book.

And I thank heaven for my editor Leslie Schnur and the wonderful gang at Dell, and for my agent Kris Dahl and her assistant Dorothea Herrey at ICM.

CONTENTS

"If a man does not keep pace with his companions, perhaps it is because he hears a different drummer. Let him step to the music which he hears, however measured or far away."

HENRY DAVID THOREAU

Introduction

What would it take to make you really happy?

Would you have to be a huge financial success? Have the biggest house in town? Own your own helicopter? That's what advertisers tell us is the key to happiness.

Well, I think they're totally wrong.

Unless you have some innate, personal love of big houses or helicopters, don't let yourself buy into someone else's idea of the good life. If you do, you're in for a big letdown. Because no one but you has any idea what will make you happy.

What you love is as unique to you as your fingerprints. You need to know that because *nothing will make you really happy but doing what you love.* Just look at people who are actually living their dreams. You can see a calm focus in their eyes and patience in their actions. They know they're in the right place, doing the right thing.

I know a man who loves getting up in the morning, going out into his kennel and checking on his Jack Russell terriers. "I can't wait to get out there and say hello, see if they're okay, have them say hello to me."

I know a fourth grade art teacher who says, "I love to create an atmosphere that makes the children open up. You should see what they paint. I think they're the greatest artists in the world!"

And I know the owner of a cafe who loves to go to work every day. "There's nothing like having your own place. I like everything about it, grinding the coffee, talking to customers, even wiping the counter."

Somewhere inside yourself you know what you love, too. You

1

dream of starting your own business, or traveling the world, or finding the right mate; you wish you could ride the horses on your own ranch, or lead your party to victory as a senator; or go diving off the Great Barrier Reef with a fabulous underwater camera.

Or maybe you don't know exactly what your dreams are, but you can sense them somewhere deep within you. Even when they're not clearly defined, they're never far away. As a matter of fact, dreams are almost impossible to get rid of. They trouble and tempt you. They keep reminding you that you're not satisfied with your life, that something crucial is missing.

And that's very lucky for you. If your dreams didn't trouble you, you'd forget them entirely. That's what you were trained to do. Most of us were told that we'd have to make daunting sacrifices to go after what we love: we'd have to abandon our lives and live in garrets or on mountaintops and we'd have to have talent a thousand times greater than anyone else, because only special people make it. Whenever we dream out loud, we're criticized for being foolish by people who really have no idea how special we are. As a result, we crush our dreams without giving them half a chance. Whenever we begin thinking, "I'd love to travel," or "I'd love to paint," we quickly rattle off all the reasons why we can't: "I don't have the money, I don't have the time, I might not be good enough . . ."

How do I know all this? Because I'm just like you. In the middle of trying to survive as a single working parent with two jobs, I too watched my birthdays come and go. When my life would get quiet for a moment, I could hear the nagging voice of unfinished dreams. What were they? I didn't really know. But sometimes in the evenings after I'd put the children to bed, I'd have thoughts I never would have admitted to anyone: maybe I was special. Maybe I was supposed to be doing something remarkable. Maybe one day I'd be respected for doing what I loved.

Sometimes I'd even take a tentative step. I'd convince myself that I should be able to make something of myself, no matter what the odds. After all, we create our own reality, don't we? All I had to do was believe in myself and I could do anything, right? At least, that's what it said in every self-improvement book I'd ever read—and I had read them all. Just think positive, tough it out, never quit. If you can't follow through on a dream, the problem is all in your head. Change your thinking.

Pardon me, but when I write those words I start getting all steamed up because believing them made me feel like a complete failure. If those phrases work for you, more power to you, but they have never worked for me. I can't tell myself how to think. I can't do just anything I set my mind to (trust me on that one—I've been trying to learn Latin for years). As for quitting, I'm famous for it. I still fall off diets with stunning regularity.

I say this now almost proudly, but back then I was certain that I was doomed to failure. I'd watch those TV commercials that show people with perfect bodies happily exercising on machines, and I'd listen to the promises that I could look perfect too if I'd only buy that machine and use it. But I didn't fall for the ads because I had tried a dozen times to exercise and by now I knew persistance wasn't my long suit. I'd lose motivation, or I'd get lonely; I was often in a lousy mood, I'd look for a million things to do besides exercise. Maybe someone out there could follow the instructions they give but not me. I knew myself too well to even try.

Anyway, maybe what I loved wasn't so important after all. Maybe my dreams wouldn't really make me happy. Maybe this feeling that I'm special and that my dreams should matter was foolish, even neurotic. Maybe dreams are just that—dreams and nothing more.

So I sighed and decided to give up. Obviously, I didn't have the right stuff in me. If I couldn't even stick with exercise, what was the point in trying for anything really big? When you don't have what it takes, you just settle for less.

Oh, was I wrong. It takes my breath away to think about how close I came to closing the door on all my cherished dreams. But one day a question lodged itself in my mind and refused to go away.

If I was such a failure, how had I managed to finish school and hold jobs and raise kids? Those were all hard to do. They required continued persistence over many years! And I had done them! How? Not with positive thinking or believing in myself, or improving my attitude one bit, that's for sure. I must have accomplished those feats some other way.

I felt on the verge of a very big discovery. I was so excited that day I called all my startled friends and shouted into the phone, "We can all have what we want and we don't have to change at all, and we don't have to have the right attitude or anything! Isn't that astounding? We've all been sold a bill of goods! I'll get back to you on this!"

Obviously I had my own way of accomplishing hard things. Determined to design a program that would suit me, I sat down and carefully took apart every belief I ever had about what it takes to achieve a dream. So I wasn't perfect. So what? I wanted a life I would love anyway, and I wanted it as soon as possible.

And I was willing to rethink every assumption I'd ever had to get that life.

What I learned changed my course forever.

One by one I went through every rule I'd been taught: ignore your feelings unless they're good ones, forget what you love and be practical enough to go after what you're skilled at, never doubt yourself, you're in charge of how you see the world, self-discipline is a must, willpower and determination are essential, never let fear stop you, scold yourself when you quit, always know exactly what you want . . . the list was long. And for me, impossible.

Knowing what I know now I can only be grateful it was. Because if I had been able to follow those rules, I'd have talked myself into all kinds of unnecessary foolishness that doesn't match the way I work. I'd have wasted a lot of time and could have done myself real harm. You see, those rules don't work for me in just the way a size four shoe doesn't fit me. There's nothing wrong with me, and maybe there's nothing wrong with the shoe, either. It was simply made for someone else.

Like those exercise machines, self-improvement programs don't take into consideration how we feel about exercise, or what motivates us. They don't know what demoralizes us, they don't know how we organize our time or what—if anything—we do for support. They don't know a thing about me or you, and they don't care. Why should they? We're supposed to change. Not the program.

But study after study confirms the terrible truth: *changing your temperament is probably impossible.* At one time I would have considered that the worst news in the world. After all, if we can't change ourselves, how can we change our lives? Do we now have to settle for lives we don't love, and sigh every time we have another birthday? And ache every time another year comes to a close?

Get ready for a shocker: *the fact that most of us can't change means there's nothing but hope.* If you or I were the only people who had trouble with those rules for success, the problem would be ours. But if *most* people have trouble following them, *maybe the rules are the problem.* Assuming that the same program will work for all of us is like feeding oats to a tiger or birdseed to a horse.

If you're ever in a big room where everyone is roaring out positive affirmations, look around. Some people are obviously inspired. I get a headache. Have you ever heard the saying, "When the going gets tough, the tough get going?" Some people do their best when they're challenged that way. I get tired.

And still I accomplish a lot in my life. And so do you.

Your style of achieving goals might be radically different from mine. That's fantastically good news. That means the reason most of us haven't been able to run after our dreams is that we were wearing the wrong size shoes. All we have to do is discover what fits us, and chances are we'll do just fine.

That was my biggest discovery—but it wasn't the only one.

I'm so glad I woke up that day and stopped blaming myself. Because one by one the pieces all fell into place. I had no reason to be ashamed of my grand dreams or believing I might be special. Far from it.

I realized that dreams are astoundingly important. They keep nagging you because *you're supposed to fulfill them.* When you sense you're special, you're not neurotic or grandiose. Something inside you is calling to you and *you have to listen.* When you love to do something, that means you have a gift for it. Every time.

And when you're gifted at something, *you have to do it.*

That's why you have to pay close attention to what you love, and never listen to anyone who tells you to be practical too early in the game. You don't have to quit your job and mortgage your house, but you do have to turn those dreams over and give them a careful look. If you don't pay attention to what you love, you could overlook your greatest gifts! That love is the surefire indicator of hidden gifts, *and it is the only way to find them.* Skills don't count. They're just abilities that were useful enough to be developed. Gifts often haven't had the chance to be developed and because of that we're fooled into thinking they don't exist. But the pleasure you feel when you see a subtle color, or dance to your favorite music, or read a certain kind of book is like a bell being rung by your gifts saying, "Here we are!"

You arrived on this planet loaded with gifts and talent, seeing the world in a way no one ever saw it before. Nature meant for you to use that unique vision as surely as she meant for a fish to swim or a bird to fly. These gifts are as much yours as the color of your eyes. You didn't choose them and you didn't create them. Just as their name implies, they are "gifts."

And they come with a mandate: "Use us!"

And that's exactly what I want you to do. Here at the beginning of this book, I want you to do what I did—put away all your former notions of what it takes to get a life you love and start over, from scratch. The lessons in this book will show you how to create a program expressly suited to you, based on who you are and what you need. The battle to change yourself into something you are not is over. *That's why this program will work where others haven't.* Because it's right for you, it will carry you like wind and waves carry a boat.

Here are the only three principles you will need:

First—*You are one of a kind.* The world will never see anyone like you again. You have unique perceptions and your own contribution to make. Your gifts are coded into your genes. You're born with them and they're as unique as everything else about you. If you base what you do on your gifts, you will be unusually good at it. But only you can discover your gifts because only you know what you love.

Second—*You will never be happy unless you are using your gifts.* You were born to use them. Your dreams are based on those gifts, and if you don't try to fulfill your dreams, you will be discontented and sad. It won't matter how else you try to fill the emptiness. Your hands are longing to pick up the right material and go to work doing what you are gifted at.

Look at all the people who use their gifts—woodcarvers and surgeons, photographers or boat builders or naturalists—you can sense their quiet confidence, their unselfconscious steadiness, a rightness in their lives. You know deep down that could be you.

Third—*You don't have to change yourself to change your life.* No personality makeovers are necessary. You are fine just as you are. No major sacrifices are necessary, either. There is always a realistic way to fulfill any dream. There has never been a dream that you can't have—at least, not the heart of it, not the part you love the most.

To get it you won't need to practice self-discipline or self-improvement either.

You will need to find out what motivates you, so you'll treat yourself right. You may need praise, or you may need competition. You may need special triggers to help you remember what you're learning. You may need your own kind of affirmation—or no affirmations at all. I'll show you new ways to overcome the feeling of loneliness that so often accompanies the first steps of going after a dream and also teach you some tricks for getting know-how, insider information, advice, and practice.

Whatever you need, you're going to get. That's how you'd treat anyone else if you sincerely wanted them to succeed, and that's how you're going to treat yourself.

You're in for some big insights about why it's been so hard to stick to any resolution. You see, the problem was never laziness or lack of character—it was something our biology brought to the party—resistance. You need to understand resistance well to know how to get around it. The methods you'll learn are different from anything you'd ever imagine.

Then you're going to try out all your new knowledge in a trial run, just as you would if you were about to climb a mountain or go deep-sea diving. And then you're going after your big dream.

If you're not sure you even know what your big dream is yet, don't worry. Every lesson will bring you closer to finding it.

One more thing. Every exercise you'll be asked to do in these lessons has been designed for normal human beings, not motion picture heroes. You can't know it yet, but this program is different from any you've ever seen—you'll find that out in the first lesson. This program will work because you're going to tailor it to fit you perfectly. Failure has been built out of the system—and if you don't think that's possible, you're in for the surprise of your life. You're about to discover what it means to be unstoppable.

Now, what about improving yourself? Well, it's entirely unnecessary, but it's going to happen anyway. You see, going after what you love improves you. It makes you feel energized and purposeful and confident—all without any work on your part. You'll become more generous and flexible. You'll become a better person without doing one self-improvement exercise. It comes with the territory.

Because having your dreams fulfilled can be far more therapeutic than having them analyzed.

And not fulfilling your dreams will be a loss to the world, because the world needs everyone's gifts—yours and mine. As a freedom fighter named Ben Linder once said, "Anything you can do needs to be done, so pick up the tool of your choice and get started." He was talking about helping other people, but every time you pick up "the tool of your choice," even if you think you're only pleasing yourself, you're helping all of us. We all depend on the gifts of others—of teachers and painters and poets and inventors and businesspeople—and it's only right that we give our best back.

So prepare yourself to go the whole distance—all the way to a life you're going to love. You'll need a notebook, two packs of 3 × 5 index cards—one plain and one in your favorite color—and a pencil. Then just sit down, open the pages and one by one take the steps I've outlined for you. You'll find them human-size steps, not giant steps. They don't require special skills or special thinking—just a little time and some writing. You're going to enjoy every one of them. They're easy and fun and unlike any exercises you've ever done before.

Just find a quiet place to read and start turning the pages. If you read the lessons and follow the simple instructions in each chapter, you're going to get an unexpected reward for it.

You'll be living the life you love before you even finish this book.

That's a promise.

L E S S O N   O N E

What Motivates You?

"Anything that is not graded is vicarious at MIT, because you need the pressure of the other students and the quizzes and the graded problem sets to force you to absorb the mountain of data presented."

PEPPER WHITE, *THE IDEA FACTORY*

✦

Carl Reiner: "What was the main mode of transportation 2000 years ago?"
Mel Brooks: "Fear."

THE 2000-YEAR-OLD MAN

Nobody makes you go after a dream. It's not like doing your schoolwork or paying your rent. No one is waiting for you to realize all your talents. You're on your own. Fulfilling your own potential, realizing your gifts, these are the only important things in our culture that are left entirely to you. Rarely does someone help you search for your hidden gifts, or give you the same guidance to develop them that you would get learning to read or do math or play football or drive a car. That's why we all have a very hard time following through on our impulses to write a novel, learn a new language, or try out photography.

All the same, most of us have made some attempts to try to develop our talents. The urge to follow your gifts never quite goes away. Many of us have flirted with our dreams, taking a class or two in something we loved. Most of the time we were unable to find the motivation to follow through and turn these beginnings into a serious commitment—far less a career. Some people seem to have the drive to be unstoppable, to take themselves seriously, to never give up. They are the envy of us all. So how do we become like them?

I was always taught that you had to develop character, to be hard on yourself and not give in to laziness or fear if you were going to achieve a goal. But no matter how I tried to tough things out and find the willpower to follow my dream, I usually lost heart and gave up. I noticed that some people responded well to rewards: if they were able to lose ten pounds they promised themselves a new outfit. Other people seemed galvanized by criticism or put-downs; they took them as a dare. If someone had said to them, "You'll never climb that mountain," they set their jaws and started to climb.

And that's how I realized that when it comes to motivation, we're all different. You may respond to one kind and the person next to you responds to something completely different. I found that very reassuring. That meant that there was hope for all of us, that somewhere there was some kind of motivation that would work for me. And it made perfect sense: since we're all unique, one of a kind, then every one of us needs different kinds of motivation.

Of course, that means we have to find them for ourselves. Who else can do it?

Lesson One:
What Motivates You?

I used to love making resolutions on New Year's Day or on my birthday. It always put me in a fantastic mood. A fresh start feels so invigorating. Each time I was just sure I'd really buckle down and exercise every day, or write that novel, or get organized once and for all. Finally, I told myself, I would have an orderly life, fulfill my creative potential, be in charge. I would look to the heroes of our society, the megasuccesses and renew my vow to be like them, disciplined and focused, never entertaining a doubt or a negative thought.

Sound familiar?

And have you found, like me, that you always break those promises to yourself? That your resolve melts and you turn back into who you were before that great, invigorating mood filled you?

If this is you, then welcome to the club. Whatever magical energy or character trait propelled the megasuccesses, it is clear that most of us don't have it, because everyone I know is just like me, filled with tales of resolutions broken and talent not fulfilled.

Obviously people like us make up a very big market. In fact, a major industry has emerged, devoted to cheerleading us into positive thinking and self-confidence, believing in ourselves, talking ourselves into being winners. And no matter how many books and programs appear, there is always a need for more of them. How strange that so many people don't drive themselves to success. What's the matter with us?

Years ago I knew I was going to have a problem building a life

I would love if something didn't change. For a while, I thought maybe most of us didn't deserve to succeed, that maybe we didn't want our dreams badly enough. Then I thought maybe our Puritan forefathers were right—humans are born with bad stuff in them, streaks of laziness and weakness, negative thinking and worse.

But that just didn't make sense. Why would a species produce so many individuals who were programmed wrong? Why would nature allow the survival of creatures who didn't use their abilities? How can it be that most of us will fall by the wayside? Something seemed cockeyed about that thinking.

That's when I began to get suspicious. I was accustomed to thinking that *I* lacked the character traits that made people successful, but how could it be that almost *everyone* did, too?

Whenever we study animals in the wild, we invariably assume that there is some logical reason for their behavior. We never assume they're naughty or stupid or trying to create trouble for themselves. Instead of rebuking or trying to change animals, we pay attention, trying to figure out the cause for any behavior we don't understand. I decided to look at myself with the same respect I'd give any other animal and assume that if I do something foolish maybe there's a logical reason for it.

I racked my brain. How did I ever accomplish anything in the past? What made me finish college when I have such a hard time studying? Why did I work so many hours to take care of my kids? What had motivated *me*?

Not how did Donald Trump or Sir Edmund Hillary do it. How did *I* do it?

And then I realized what it was. I had motivated myself all right, but I'd invented half the methods and handpicked the others. Without knowing it, I had instinctively put together a combination of motivational techniques that sidestepped my inability to discipline myself, or think positively, or change my attitude.

You see, I'm a very interesting case. Twenty years later, with no noticeable self-improvement, I have managed to get myself a great life! I still can't stay on a diet or an exercise program, I can't learn a language or a musical instrument, much as I want to—I can't even make myself try very hard.

And yet, I've built a life I love.

I do the work I love, I live in a place that makes me happy, and I have good people around me. I've done some traveling. I even got successful. I'm working on my fifth book, and people tell me I've been very helpful to them; I'm managing to pay my bills. That's pretty much my whole list for a good life.

But, if you have to improve your character to get a good life, how did I get one? I've had a lot of good luck, but none of it would have come my way if I hadn't worked hard over a long period of time. And I've had my share of disasters that I somehow recovered from. What motivated me? Was it all that self-discipline stuff they say you need? Did I "go for the burn"? Did I hang on like a pit bull and never entertain a moment of self-doubt?

I did not.

I complained loudly every time something went wrong. I wish I had a dollar for every negative thought I've harbored in my heart. And self-discipline has never worked for me. It seems like a contradiction in terms. I've always figured it was the job of other people—parents, teachers, the Department of Motor Vehicles—to do the discipline part, while my "self" did things that were more fun. I respond well to "outside" rules: I cross the street on the green light and obey most laws. I show up at work.

I just don't respond well to "inside" rules. I can't drink eight glasses of water or write a page every day and I can't change my attitude. Whenever I can get away with it, I avoid things that scare me or that are hard to do because I much prefer those that are enjoyable or easy. Of course, I'm as capable of feeling guilt and shame as the next person, so I don't always go out and have fun.

Sometimes I sit home, feel guilty and ashamed, watch TV—and still avoid hard work.

But when it comes to going after my dreams, I found out how to do it.

And so can you. Look back into your past and ask yourself the same question I did: What motivated you? You too have accomplished a lot in your life. Even as a baby you were amazing. You learned how to walk and speak your first language. You went to school, got involved in a sport or a hobby, held a job, or raised a family. Look at what you've accomplished and you will find, as I did, *that you have your own energy source.* You too have instinctively developed ways that motivate you to swing into action and get things done.

You can use those same ways to create a life you love.

Notice I'm talking about improving your *life,* not your *self.* It may not be necessary to improve yourself at all. I'm still the same as I always was, with one exception: my frame of mind is greatly improved. Not because I try to think positively—I'm no good at that—but because there's nothing like a good life to improve your disposition.

I want you to forget everything you've absorbed about what motivates captains of industry, famous athletes, or other culture heroes. Instead, I want you to start from scratch building a life that fits you as you are—not as someone told you you're supposed to be. You see, nothing is wrong with you.

Something is wrong with the messages you've been given.

Most change experts sincerely feel they have the answer. A tough coach barking that you're the lowest form of life on this planet, or a gentle soothing guru telling you to fill your mind with only the most healing thoughts honestly believe their method will help everybody. Well, those methods may help some people some of the time but they leave many of us behind—because they were developed by experts who left out what's most important: *who we are.*

You see, there is no one "right" method for motivating people to change.

I remember a scene from the film *An Officer and a Gentleman,* in which Morgan Freeman announces to a line of raw recruits that he expects half of them to fail. In fact he plans to do everything he can to make them crack, because only those that remain deserve to be pilots. As I watched, I thought, "the only recruits who will make it through that system will be those with a talent for taking abuse." Now, maybe that's what's required in the military. I can't pretend to judge military training. But I have a big problem with this method when it comes to the nonmilitary world.

Our culture often equates the ability to endure punishment with excellence. We believe that if you don't have the guts to suffer, you don't deserve to win. For damaged, bitter characters like the one played by Richard Gere, this philosophy may really be a lifesaver. But what about the rest of us? A lot of people with other kinds of genius get thrown on the trash heap when endurance is the main measure of worthiness. I wonder how many gifted people are walking around thinking they don't have what it takes because they couldn't make it through gym class, or a punishing college experience, or some other endurance-based change model.

This model is standard for men in our culture, but it affects women, too. Even a woman who has raised children with support and understanding will apply the "male military standard" to herself and feel like a failure when she comes up short. We're all taught that real winners can take abuse.

Many such yardsticks exist in our culture and we're trained to measure ourselves against them no matter how little they apply to us. It's a funny thing: when the shoe doesn't fit, we think we're supposed to wear it anyway.

It's time to stop that kind of thinking. When too many people flunk a program, something's wrong with the program. If you tried in the past to go after your dreams—and you failed—*there's an excellent chance that it wasn't your fault.* You probably were using techniques that were designed for someone else.

Sometime in our childhood, we split ourselves in two and take on the roles of both top sergeant and recruit. We set the goals, challenge ourselves to meet them, and try to meet that challenge. We take over our own boot camp program. We no longer need anyone else to scold us—we do it ourselves.

When you think about it, taking on both roles could be a very great opportunity for us. Instead of requiring ourselves to have an iron jaw and an ego of steel, we could try to teach ourselves with kindness and compassion. Maybe we could put a carrot ahead to entice us instead instead of driving ourselves like tired horses. Or maybe we'd conclude that we do our best work in a team getting lots of encouragement, surrounding ourselves with friends every time we go after something difficult.

Doesn't that sound like a great idea? Well, it's in your hands to do it. You're finally in a position to put everything you need in your corner to help yourself win. You no longer have to try to motivate yourself in ways that don't work. You can come up with great alternatives—whatever works best for you.

That's what Lesson One is going to teach you—the alternatives: how to discover just what it will take to make *you* unstoppable. Your days of off-the-rack programs are over. Like off-the-rack clothes, they are designed to fit the "average human." But when it comes to your dreams, your talents, your potential, there is nothing "average" about you. What do you need to coax out your best work? Find that and you'll know the secret to your success.

That's the right way, the only way, to carry a dream the whole distance.

So let's get right into it. Pull out your notebook and get your pencil ready.

Exercise 1: Three Stories and a Quiz

Story 1:

Joe has an interview, and though he should be ready, he's frightened and unsure of himself. If he doesn't get some confidence, he's going to blow it. One friend tells him he'll do fine. Another tells him the job doesn't matter anyway. A third says he's a sissy for being so scared. What would you tell him? Open your notebook and write your answer, then see what some other people wrote.

Mary: My first impulse is to give him a big hug and remind him how great he is.

Rich: I'd tell him to go for a ten mile run. I'd go with him. Give him some exercise so he gets a good night's sleep. He needs some company to get his mind off it.

Nelson: I'd tease him and make him laugh at himself. It's not the end of the world.

Story 2:

Annette wants to write a novel more than anything in the world. She's made some attempts, but always stops. "I know I should write every morning, but I can't find the time. When I do, I think what I write is boring. I'm afraid I'm just mediocre."

What would you tell Annette? Be sure to write it in your notebook before you read how other people answered so you'll catch your first reaction. Then look at what other people said.

Melanie: Go to a class! She needs a teacher! Somebody to show her the ropes.

Marty: Get a little writers' group going and have everybody bring in something they wrote every week to read aloud. It gives you somebody to do it for. And it takes all the concentration off yourself.

Gage: I'd tell her to forget it, that she probably doesn't have what it takes. If that didn't make her mad enough to write, nothing would.

Story 3:

Paula wants to find a job working with animals, but she doesn't want to be a veterinarian. She can't imagine another way to make a living working with animals so she's about to give up. What would you tell her to do?

Phil: I'd introduce her to someone I know who's making a fortune breeding horses in Kentucky.

Annette: I'd try to give her a lot of ideas, like being a dog walker, or working in a zoo or the animal shelter—whatever I could think of. And then I'd tell her to go find out about these things, by visiting those places or reading about them in a magazine or the public library.

Take a look at your answers, and the answers of other people. What do they reveal? Obviously we don't know much about what would motivate Joe, Annette, or Paula to go after their dreams, but we might know something about what motivates the people who answered the questions: they probably gave the kind of help they'd like to receive. What about you? Look at your answers. Does some part of you need the advice or help you'd have given Joe, Annette, and Paula? If it does, you're starting to uncover some clues about what you need to motivate you.

Now let's take another angle.

Exercise 2: Two Stories About You

Story 1:

A: NO HELP WAS ON THE WAY.

Think back to your childhood. Was there a time you wanted to do something but didn't know how to make it happen? Did you ask for help and get unhelpful responses? Or did you not even try because you knew what to expect? In your notebook, tell the story. What did you want and what happened when you asked for help? If you didn't ask for help, tell why.

Eugene: I wanted to go out for track in junior high, but I was a fat kid. It was pretty stupid I guess. I asked the coach and he looked at me like I was a slug. I think he said I'd have to work so hard it wouldn't be worth it or something. He didn't like me.

Lynn: I did some writing for the school paper and I had a math teacher, a tough lady, who seemed to like what I wrote although she didn't say much. One day she read a column, I think it was my fifth or sixth, and she called me in after class and said she was very disappointed in me, that the last column was below what she expected of me. I wanted to die. I didn't know what she meant and I didn't know how to write the way she wanted, so I never wrote another column for the paper.

What did you write? Take a look at your story, at what happened to you. Now pick up your pen because I want you to write one more thing.

B: YOU TO THE RESCUE.

Imagine as an adult you witnessed the whole story you just wrote. Imagine the child sat down alone and you walked over, deciding to help. What would you say to him or her?

Eugene: I'd have helped that kid. I'd have said "It'll be hard but you can do it. Here's what you should eat to lose weight, and here's when you should come out to run, and I'll be there to show you how." I'd have helped him out because it's really great when a kid wants to do something like that. It's really stupid to discourage a kid who wants to do better.

Lynn: I'd have been very gentle because if she was like me, she got very little support at home. I'd have said, "This is really good writing. Would you like me to show you some writing tricks?" And if she liked that, I'd continue. But if she got really sensitive, you know what I'd do? I'd just tell her she was great, and I'd be her biggest fan and I'd never criticize a thing. I'd make her feel smart and safe, even if her writing wasn't perfect. And then when she got more sure of herself, she'd see what was wrong on her own. I guess that teacher couldn't have known how incredibly sensitive I was. She never offered to show me what she meant, or to help me. It took me twenty years before I could write anything I was willing to show anyone. That was such a waste."

Take a look at your answer now, and notice how it makes you feel to remember the story you told. It's so clear what kind of help you needed as a child and sad to remember how rarely you got it. Without support you probably thought, as most children do, that something was wrong with you, or that what you wanted was foolish. Do you start to see how much of your self-blame is misplaced?

There's a right way and a wrong way to motivate runners and writers—of any age. I don't want to imagine how much talent has been wasted because of these bad moves on the part of adults. Of course, even well-meaning people can make mistakes. We don't always understand very clearly what other people need from us. But you can start to discover what *you* need and find a way to get it for yourself.

Now, do the second part of Exercise 2.

Story 2:

In your notebook, write about a time when you got exactly the help you needed. Think back. If you got the right kind of help more than once, write down every time and describe the kind of help you got and what the result was.

Betsy: I was in college in this grueling music appreciation class. It was harder than a math class, and I just couldn't get it. I couldn't read music and I couldn't hear what the teacher was trying to point out. The day before the final exam I thought I was finished. It was a clear "F." And then at the end of the class this girl came up to me. I hardly knew her but she was so kind. She said she and some other students were getting together to cram for the exam and would I like to come? Of course, I jumped at the chance. Well we stayed up all night, and the way I remember it, they worked mostly on me, all of them. Testing me, explaining things, just getting me ready. It was the most amazing experience I ever had. I got a "B" on my final exam thanks to their help. I almost cry when I think of it. I wish I could find that girl and thank her again.

Bill: I wanted to act, but I had given up all thoughts of doing it. It seemed so time-consuming and although I loved acting, I wasn't very sure of myself. My family had never wanted me to be an actor, so I became an accountant. Well, this therapist told me I should read some Shakespeare, just a few lines, every night before I went to sleep. It changed everything. It made me remember how much I loved theater, and I started doing play readings at home, inviting other actors. Now the theater is back in my life and it makes me very happy. The therapist knew just the right thing to say—start small. If she'd told me to go back to acting school, or out on auditions, I wouldn't have done it. I was too unsure of myself.

What happened to you? Did you ever get the right kind of help?

Now, look over the last two exercises. Are you beginning to

see in your answers what would be the best way to motivate you? That means you're ready to do some grading.

Exercise 3: Write a Report Card

Now you can begin to design a motivational package that's tailor-made for you. On the report card below is a listing of all the methods I know of that are supposed to help us stick to our resolutions. I'm sure you're familiar with most of them, maybe you've even tried a few. How well did they work for you? If you think something's missing from the list, add it. I want you to rate them for their effectiveness. It's going to be your turn to do the grading.

But first, let me explain what I mean by some of the words on this list.

"Shaming" is when you try to motivate yourself by telling yourself that you're inferior, for example, that you'll be motivated to diet if you take off all your clothes and look in the mirror. Would this method make you stick to a diet? If it would, "Shaming" gets an "A." If it sent you straight to the refrigerator for consolation, "Shaming" gets an "F." If it succeeded in slowing down your candy bar consumption a little bit, it gets a "C."

Where "Shaming" implies that you're beneath reproach, "Scolding" implies that you're simply bad because you broke your promises to yourself. A scold sounds like this: "Look what you've done. How could you be so stupid? You're definitely a bad person." In the old days, you'd get rapped on the knuckles with a ruler while you were being scolded. If this works for you, it gets high grades. If not, give it an "F."

"Lecturing" is a little different. First of all, lecturing usually goes on for a long time and second, it pretends to be teaching something, such as "Do I have to tell you that if you don't do your homework you'll never get anywhere? When I was your age I got up at five A.M. and walked ten miles in the dark. Look at the Jones boy, he's doing so well . . ." etc. Some of us keep a litany like this going in our heads for a long time. If lecturing yourself gets you back on track, it deserves an "A." If it doesn't, it's a time waster and should be given an "F."

Some people swear by "Competition." It means you look at other people and try to beat them. Runners often swear by this one. Many of them say they always run faster when someone is ahead of them, or gaining on them from behind. How about you? Does competition help you or discourage you?

A cousin of competition, and a funny one at that, is "Revenge." A friend of mine described it this way: "All I have to do to succeed at something is imagine how happy my enemies would be if I failed. That makes me nuts. I can't stand it! And then I think of how they'd hate it if I succeeded and I just smile inside and get going!"

"Who are your enemies, for heaven's sake?" I asked her, astonished.

"Everybody who was ever mean to me or didn't like me," she answered.

You be the judge. This method is as legitimate as any other. My friend should give it an "A." What about you?

On the list I include "Fear." That means someone outside you threatens real reprisals: "Keep your commitments or I'll see that you pay the price—I'll fire you, or audit your books, or refuse to refund your money, or tell your mom." Incidentally, don't laugh at Fear. It works great for me! I give it an "A!"

Some people try to keep to their resolutions by repeating "affirmations," like "I deserve to be healthy," or "I am a good person." Affirmations hardly ever work for me for more than a few minutes. After that, I don't believe what I'm saying. Still, they're always worth a try. So I give affirmations a "D," while other people give them an "A+." Do what's right for you.

There's still another interesting method out there these days. A friend of mine calls it "Pain-driven." One success program persuaded him that if he didn't absolutely hate his present situation, he would never change it. He walked around for months trying to hate his life as a way of motivating himself to make more money, but aside from needing money, my friend has a great life! He has a wonderful marriage, and he does work he loves. This method made him miserable and it didn't work so finally he gave it an "F" and went looking for a better way to motivate himself.

One of my clients said he has often tried to rise above the day-to-day urgencies of life by trying to connect to an inner peace and the energy in the universe. He hoped it would help him stick to his goals. He called that "Spirituality."

"It was very pleasant and calming, it made me feel good, but it didn't help motivate me very much." He gave it an "Incomplete."

I know someone who is motivated by believing in "Reincarnation." She says, "I'm determined to get my life right this time so I don't have to come back." It works for her! But another person I know said that if she believed in reincarnation she'd never feel any urgency to do anything.

Some people try to empower themselves by believing it's possible to "create your own reality." In other words, obstacles are only illusions and shouldn't stop you. Such people feel very empowered by this belief. Others feel that this viewpoint is a heavy burden, as though every bad thing that ever happened was their own fault. It can cut both ways: believing you create reality might give you the courage to get out of a bad situation, or it might make you blame yourself for acts of God. You decide.

Got the picture? The other items on the list should explain themselves. Also, be sure to add anything I may have overlooked.

Now start grading. Whatever works for you, gets an "A." *That's the kind of motivation you must have if you're going to go after the good life.* Any item on the list that you're not sure of needs a review before you use it on yourself.

Most important, whatever has not given you good results, *flunk it soundly.* Give it an "F" and forget it. It may have done wonders for someone else, but it wasn't right for you. And when you use motivational techniques that are wrong for you, you can injure yourself. Remember those stories you wrote and the ones you read at the beginning of this chapter. The wrong treatment makes all the difference.

The right treatment makes all the difference, too. You can see that now, can't you?

You can put the grades right in this book if you like. I've also left a column for your comments, so you can briefly explain why you gave the grade. When you look back on this page in the future, your comments will help you remember what you were thinking about.

Method	Grade	Comments
Spirituality		
Scolding		
Guilt		
Lecturing		
Competition		
Revenge		
Fear		
Shaming		
Taking a class		
Praying		
Dares		
Positive thinking		

Method	Grade	Comments
Getting lots of praise		
Reincarnation		
Repeating affirmations		
Pain-driven		
Creating your own reality		
Promising yourself a reward		
Getting help from buddies		
Starting small		
Other		

There you are. I hope you're starting to understand where the blame belongs for many of your past defeats. Nothing was wrong with you. You were using the wrong motivational methods on yourself and they held you back as surely as trying to run a race with a stone in your shoe. Don't you agree that you deserve another chance? Let's see how well you go after a dream when you're using the right tools. That's how winners really win: *they find out what they need to do their best work—and they get it.*

And that's what you can do now that you're knowledgeable enough to be in charge of your own motivational program. If you need praise, instruct your friends to praise you. If you need to be scolded, set up a buddy system and you can help each other. Your buddy can scold you (if that works for you) and you can remind your buddy that her enemies will love it if she fails (if that works for her). If you need deadlines, set them for yourself and write them in your calendar; or promise someone you'll deliver on a certain date. If you work best in a team, pull some people into your project to work with you, and if you need competition, set it up for yourself. Never again judge what you need or assume that you should be able to win using someone else's motivational style. That's over. *You're the expert on what you need, so listen to yourself.*

I hope this lesson has been something of a revelation. You've learned it well if your eyes are opened to how many motivational styles exist—and if you get it loud and clear that you can only use those that are right for you.

**◆ MEMORY DECK ALERT:
MOTIVATIONAL REPORT CARD**

Now I want you to open the pack of blank 3 × 5 cards I mentioned earlier. You're about to create a Memory Deck. In it you'll write whatever is most important for you to remember. Whenever you have a spare moment during your day, just pull out the deck and thumb through it at random, reading what you've written. Old ways of thinking die hard and new ones get lost easily, so you'll need this easy method to reinforce what you learn here.

Take out a white 3 × 5 card from your Memory Deck and write a one word heading on one side: "Yes." Under it, list only the methods you gave an "A," such as "Taking a class," or "Promising yourself a reward," or "Getting praise." At the bottom of the card draw an arrow pointing down to remind you to turn the card over. Head the other side of the card "No," and write all the methods from the list that you graded "F," such as "Scolding," "Competition," etc.

Now put the card back in the Memory Deck, wrap a rubber band around it, and keep it with you while you read on.

Congratulations. You have just learned Lesson One: Treat yourself like a champion and soon you will be one.

LESSON TWO

Gather Your Allies

"When the warriors from our tribes would lay themselves down to sleep, they would gather their allies around them to keep watch over them, for the soul leaves the body at night to travel in the land of dreams and the body cannot protect itself."

DAN GEORGE, TLINGET TRIBESMAN,
HAINES, ALASKA, 1959

Now that you know what motivates you, you'll be able to go on your great adventure. But the unknown can be frightening. You need two things now that you didn't need when you were stuck: courage and safety. Our society isn't very good at filling those needs. It's assumed that we'll somehow find them inside of ourselves.

America is a country of individualists and self-starters with a tradition of striking out on their own to seek their fortune. The world our grandparents came from was more formal. Starting something new was harder because usually there were more restrictions and rules. Families and communities typically had more control over their members and felt more justified in exercising it than we do. Traditions were established.

Today we've gotten the freedom to choose our own paths, and

31

it's been a great gift. But we've lost much of the support that existed in the old world and as a result many of us have been unwilling or afraid to take advantage of all our freedom. We've lost a lot to gain our individualism, and down deep we know it.

Companies and armies and schools know it, too. When they seriously want a job done, they create support teams and put them to work. No matter how they may preach individuality, they're too practical to depend on it totally.

Later in these lessons, when your dream starts to take shape and you seriously want a job done, you're going to learn how to create your own personal support team just as these institutions do. But to even embark on a search for your dream you're going to need a sense of safety. If you feel isolated, your survival instincts will stay on alert and you'll be stressed out. You need the courage that comes from knowing you're not alone. You need a team now, a special kind of team that can watch over you as you travel in the land of dreams—an imaginary team of allies.

What good can imaginary allies do? They can't hold the ladder while you climb up to the roof, but they can fix that lonely spot inside you that makes you feel uncertain—and uncertainty always accompanies adventures into unknown territory. Make no mistake, that's the kind of adventure you have embarked on. You're going after a life you love, using talents and gifts you may not have counted on before. No matter how you look at it, this adventure feels risky.

Native Americans understand this feeling very well. They know how to enlist the support of spirit allies. You too have spirit allies and Lesson Two will help you find them.

Lesson Two:
Gather Your Allies

M ost of us remember having someone standing by us at one time or another, when we were in trouble. Think back for a moment and find one of those memories. Maybe it was your mom stepping forward when some kid bullied you, or maybe it was your grandfather taking your side when your mom was mad at you. Your wife might have defended you at a family gathering, or your friend could have stood up for you when a teacher was unfair. No matter how rarely you've had an ally on your side, you never forget it. Somewhere in our bones, we keenly feel the difference between standing alone in times of uncertainty and having someone step forward to stand beside us.

Historically, Native Americans had no shortage of allies. It was a given that they could depend on their fellow tribespeople and any tribes they made alliances with. But they also recognized the need for spirit allies, powerful forces that they could call into service whenever they were needed. These were often the spirits of ancestors, or the animal spirits of their totems, such as the wolf, the bear, or the raven. It was believed that these spirit allies were obligated to protect their real-life children whenever they were called on—so they were completely dependable. Native Americans believed that every time they fell asleep they went on a dream journey far away into unknown lands and so every night they would gather their spirit allies together to watch over them until they returned to consciousness.

Whether or not you believe in spirits, you must admit that this

practice shows a deep understanding of human needs. If you've ever embarked on a venture of your own—going away from home as a kid or trying to learn a new language as an adult—you know what it's like to feel alone and unsure of yourself. Not because you're weak, but because those feelings are built into your biology.

All changes, even pleasant changes, are scary. Some primitive instinct within us doesn't trust the unknown. Don't believe me? Try this experiment. Walk into the lobby of an unfamiliar office building, take the nearest elevator or stairs to any floor—and step off. Walk away from the elevator, down the hall and stand there for a moment. Pay close attention to what you're feeling. You might be a bit uncomfortable because you don't know what to say if someone appears and asks why you're there. That's only reasonable. But you'll feel more than discomfort, something hard to name. A kind of animal uneasiness.

Now try the exact same experiment with a friend and notice how different you feel. Everything changes. You still don't know where you are, and you'd still feel a little embarrassed if anyone asked what you're doing there, but you now have someone to share the experience with, and your apprehensions disappear.

Having company drives away more than fear, it drives away hurt, too.

Going after a dream can make you feel like an orphan. If that sounds a bit dramatic, think about it for a moment. Anytime you leave a familiar place and head for somewhere new, you become an outsider. You're going to a place where you don't know the passwords, the customs, and chances are no one has invited you.

Why should a life we love take us to such unfamiliar worlds? Because, except for the few lucky people among us who happily fit in our parents' world, we must all leave home to follow our personal visions. We knew who we were at home, and so did our families. But they were rarely familiar with the side of us that dreams our private dreams. If your family liked to farm the land

and belong to a small community, they wouldn't understand a child who wanted to travel the world or live in a big city. They might feel their ways were being rejected, or they might feel frightened and angry that your ambitions appeared so dangerous. They might even catch a glimpse of the stranger in you, and pull away. In some profound way, you'd be on your own. You wouldn't belong at home with your family anymore, but you wouldn't belong anywhere else either.

How did we get to be so different from our families? We may speak the same language and behave in the same way, but when it comes to our most cherished dreams we move into a different arena, the arena of gifts and talents and special kinds of intelligence. These gifts are inherited characteristics. If you're a fast runner or a graceful dancer you have inherited a special sense of your body in space. If you long to paint, it's probably because you have inherited a gift for seeing the world around you in a unique way. These gifts are often not shared by any of our siblings or parents.

Genetic traits have a way of hiding for generations and then suddenly appearing unannounced in families that don't understand them. An accountant or a welder could easily find himself with a son or daughter who is a brilliant horticulturist. But to undiscerning eyes, a beginning horticulturist doesn't look anything like a horticulturist, he simply looks like an ordinary person who fools around with plants too much. I know a gifted mathematician from a family of artists who are convinced he's a failure because to them mathematics looks dull and uncreative!

Your family's negative reactions soak into your sensitive child's soul and chill you. That's when you begin to hurt inside. That's when you have the least support ever. And that's when you feel like an orphan.

And when you feel like an orphan, it's very hard to go after your dream. Most of us try to talk ourselves into a courage we don't really feel, but positive thinking and self-talk can't create a sense of safety because they are done alone. Alone, you cannot stop feeling like an orphan. Alone you cannot repair the dents that a tough world leaves on your self-esteem.

You need allies, and you need them now.

You need people who believe in you and can see the genius in you, right here at the beginning when you aren't at all sure of that genius yourself. Where are you supposed to find allies on such short notice? One day you'll be ready to go looking for real people who could be your allies and I'll give you some ideas to help you find them (see Lesson Seven, The Idea Bank).

But here at the beginning of this program, you need to create a team full of *spirit* allies just like the Native Americans do, and you should gather them around to protect you from uncertainty and sorrow as you journey after your dreams.

Perhaps we can't connect with the spiritual world as comfortably as Native Americans do, but with your imagination and your memory you can do very well. You might find that you want to keep these allies forever, even after you've gotten a real-life support team, because imaginary allies have great advantages.

Imaginary allies are as necessary as real ones

For one thing, you can pick exactly who you want. I never got Albert Einstein's consent to put his picture all over my house, but I can't imagine he'd mind keeping me company at so little cost to himself. In my billfold I have a ten-shekel note from Israel with a faded picture of Golda Meir on it, and everytime I look in there and see her strong, kind face, it gives me a touch of courage. Among the pictures I carry with me is one of my very favorite pet from years ago, a beautiful, long-haired black dog who I am convinced is a powerful and loving spirit ready to stand by me in my imagination, anytime I call her.

There's another very wonderful reason for creating spirit allies: it will give you practice asking for help—and receiving it. We
need this practice because the truth is most of us don't have much
experience with allies. Unless you're a very lucky person who
grew up surrounded by the best of buddies, you have to learn on
your own what you can expect from a truly good friend. And you
have to learn how to accept help. It's a skill that a few people have
since childhood and everyone else has to practice. If you're ever
going to be able to recognize and accept real, living allies into
your daily life, and learn how to have, and be, a good friend, you
have to lay down some new tracks. You need to understand what it
feels like to belong, to have the right to ask for help, and to feel
brave as people do when they feel safe in their souls. Practice with
imaginary allies will give you this understanding.

The first thing you need to figure out is—what do you need
from allies?

Exercise 1: What Do You Need from Your Allies?

Think for a moment and try to imagine what you would want
if you had the best allies imaginable. This could take some thought
because chances are you're not used to having a bunch of people
on your side, and you don't know what you want. Take a look at
what I came up with and maybe it will get you started.

I need my allies to:

+ like me just the way I am, so I don't have to worry about
  how to please them.
+ give me good advice (because they seem to know so
  much).

+ encourage me to stick with my dream when I feel like quitting.
+ use their influence on my behalf.
+ be like me in some important way, so I don't feel different.
+ have interesting things to say so I don't get bored.
+ believe my dreams are good and that I have the talent to attain them.
+ back me up whenever I need them.

Sounds great, doesn't it? It's only a wish list, nothing more, so don't hesitate to come up with everything you want on yours.

Write your answers on a sheet of paper in your notebook, then take a careful look at what you have written. Your list will be different from mine and from anyone else's. Do the next exercise and you'll see what I mean.

Exercise 2: Rank the Items on Your List

You may have liked everything on my list, and you certainly like everything on yours, but not all are essential. Now I'd like you to rank every entry in order of its importance to you. Write a "1" next to the most important, a "2" next to the second most important and so on. Pretend you only have room for five support roles from your allies (you don't have room for only five, of course, you have room for as many as you can think of, but for the purposes of this exercise just pretend for a moment). If you had to get rid of all the entries but five, which would go first?

Don't look now, but you are designing a personal list, the fingerprint of your personal and specific needs. *No one in the world could have written that list for you.* Only you understand what it takes for you to do your best work.

Even after you write down everything you need, however, you're going to have a hard time remembering what you wrote. You're not used to getting these needs met and this list can easily slip from your mind. That means it's time to write another card in your Memory Deck, so you can remind yourself regularly of what you need.

◆◇ MEMORY DECK ALERT

Take out a blank 3 × 5 card and head it "I need my allies to:" Then write down everything from Exercise 1 that you think you'd need from your allies. Don't stop at five, write as many as you can squeeze on both sides of your card, but write very clearly. If possible, leave some room for more entries as they occur to you in the days and weeks to come.

Now, every time you start randomly flipping through those cards, you'll find this one and be reminded of what you need from your allies. Once you know that, you have two choices, each very useful. You can understand and forgive yourself if you're not feeling strong. Or you can gather your allies, and get what you need.

Now, who do you want for your allies?

Exercise 3: Create a List of Candidates for Your Allies

Who would you want in your corner? Cast your first net wide, and pull in as many candidates as possible. Sit down with your notebook and pencil in a quiet corner where you can do some thinking for a few minutes, and get ready to write down the names of as many potential allies as you can think of.

To stretch your imagination, look at the following categories, and try to think of at least one name for each. I'll do it along with you so you can see my choices.

A person in history: Marco Polo because he loved adventure and travel. Abraham Lincoln because he seems so kind and consoling. Golda Meir, because she was earthy, wise, and compassionate. Albert Einstein because he loved to think.

Someone in your childhood: My grandfather Max because although he spoke no language I understood, we always understood each other perfectly.

A fictional character from books, movies, TV: Jo from *Little Women* because she was creative and affectionate and loved fun; Yentl (from the film of the same name) because she loved learning and dared to follow her dream; Shirley Valentine (from the film of the same name) because she was brave and funny and would be a wonderful friend. Goldie, the main character from the child's book, *Goldie the Dollmaker,* and Babette from the film *Babette's Feast,* because they are both true artists.

Living or dead heroes in your adult years: Vincent van Gogh because I love the wonderful letters he wrote his brother Theo about the French countryside, a woman whose name I don't remember, who helped children escape harm during the Second World War. An old man in a Greek village because he was so tough and patient. My beautiful black dog.

There, that's my list.

Now you make yours. Turn to a fresh sheet of paper in your notebook, date the page, and write down as many allies as you can think of. Try to imagine being face-to-face with them as you write their names. Don't be limited by my categories. Pull your allies from anywhere you like. In days to come, more names will occur to you. Write them all on the same page. Leave some space between the names so you can write a brief comment about why you chose each one, just as I did.

When you're done, read over your list and look at who you chose and what you wrote. Does it tell you anything about yourself? Mine did. It's obvious that being understood means a lot to me. That would make me feel safe and secure. I also see that I have a great need to be surrounded by interesting, independent people with strong opinions and lots of experiences. What did you notice? Take your pencil and underline the words that mean the most to you and see what they say about you.

One more thing: did you notice how warm your world felt while you were thinking about these people and writing their names? You like those people you thought of, and you're ready to believe that they like you, too. In a way, what you've been doing while you thought and wrote was meditating. I mean meditating in the older sense of the word. Not emptying your mind, but filling it, bringing you close to what you were thinking about, filling your mind with what you wrote. This kind of mind work can warm your soul.

Look back at your list of names and imagine for a moment that you're able to look into the faces of some of those people—and be prepared for a moving experience. In a moment, you're going to bring your allies into your life, your actual living space. But for now, just thinking about them, imagining you are looking into their faces will have a strong effect on you. In the rush of daily living it's easy to forget all the remarkable people, real or fictional, who have been a part of your life. But if you just imagine they are near for a moment, you will realize that anyone who ever touched your heart is always with you, patiently waiting to emanate warmth and support whenever you remember to think of them.

That's why you want to make sure you've got their names with you wherever you go.

◆ MEMORY DECK ALERT

Take out another 3 × 5 card. Head it "Allies," and write down the name of each one of them. I hope you have so many that you have to write very small. When you're finished, put the card back in your Memory Deck. Whenever you're stuck on a bus or in a waiting room, or have been put on hold on the phone, look through your cards randomly, and you'll stumble on this one. Read down the list and let your eye rest on any name it chooses. Your first impulse will select the right one. Suddenly, it will feel as though an ally has come to join you—just the one you need at that moment.

Exercise 4: Gather Your Allies Around You

To help you remember your allies through the day, you need to go about the business of settling in with them, just as you would with beloved relatives who have come to visit. The best way is to give your allies a place to perch! Look around your room and imagine where each should be. I've got a few of mine sitting in various chairs around my writing desk, because that's where I need them most. I imagine Shirley Valentine sitting cross-legged on my bed behind me with a smile on her face and a poster of Greece in her hand. Babette is sitting on my right, mopping her forehead with a dish towel, resting from her cooking chores. Where do you want to place yours?

Take out your notebook and write where you want your allies to stand or sit when you gather them. Look around your home or your work space and find a place for each one. You'll need to write down your decisions so you don't forget where you've put them.

Without a place to be, your allies won't seem as real. In the coming weeks you can try to find pictures and drawings of them, or even create your own drawing. Then you can put them in the right places and see them whenever you look up. Einstein's picture is on my bookcase, Goldie the Dollmaker looks out at me from an open book sitting on my desk near my computer. You might want to have the picture of one of your allies pinned to your lamp so you are reminded of her or him as you turn off the light, and another taped to the front door to stay with you when you go off into the day.

There. That makes them more real, doesn't it?

Exercise 5: Let Your Allies Find Their Voices

By now you might be finding your allies so real that you can almost hear them speak. What do you think they might say to you at this moment? Pretend each ally is in his or her place, and try to imagine what they are saying right now. Here's what I imagined:

Babette: An artist is never poor.

Shirley Valentine: As long as you're listening to your heart, you won't go far wrong.

Goldie: Do you have something nearby that's beautiful to look at? Beauty is very important for your soul.

Marco Polo: Finish your work and start to travel! There are worlds out there to discover!

Einstein: I think there are also worlds right here, Marco, right in her work.

Now you write down what you heard. Your first sheet might be full, so just continue onto a new one. Take some time and listen. You'll hear them.

There. Now your allies have names, places, and voices. They

are real to you and you can gather them near whenever you choose.

Wait a minute. What about some reality here!

Is some rational part of you protesting that no matter how great your imaginary allies may be, you'll never find anyone like them in the real world? Well, you may be right.

Back to reality

Will you ever be able to find real people to give you all the support you described on your list of needs? Can reality match this fantasy? Not unless you're very, very lucky. Real people have their own needs, their own problems and usually a few hang-ups—and they rarely have the time or inclination to devote themselves totally to you. *But a real-life, all-around perfect ally that devotes himself totally to you isn't necessary!* Even with imaginary allies, you only chose them for one or two of their characteristics, and you only need their company for brief moments now and then. The same goes for real allies. You don't really need huge amounts of support—just small, crucial doses.

But won't this imaginary paradise of great allies spoil you for the real world? Of course not. You know the difference between reality and fantasy. You're just enriching your reality, not replacing it. In fact, you're learning how to make your reality better.

Whenever you meet someone from now on, you're going to be alert to all those characteristics you value in your allies. You'll notice when they are missing—and when they're present. It's a real eye-opener to compare real people to ideal people. You'll find that some of your acquaintances are not behaving themselves very well—and you might even tell them so. You might also find that some people in your life who haven't been standing in the spotlight have quietly been real friends, and you'll come to value them as they deserve. So although no one human—and no one fantasy ally—can ever meet all your needs, this new awareness is sure to increase your chances of drawing quality people into your life. Practicing imaginary friendships with your allies is good experience for you.

And your imagination is a more powerful learning tool than you'd ever believe. I read a story of a professional skier who had been in an accident and was confined to bed for months. He spent hours every day with his eyes closed, imagining he was skiing on snow-covered slopes. When he was finally well and on his feet the doctors were surprised to find that his muscles had hardly deteriorated during his long bed stay. And when he was able to get back on the ski slopes, his timing was much better than anyone thought possible.

When should you call on your allies?

You don't need to practice dealing with allies for hours a day, but it's a good idea to call on them at crucial moments, just to remind yourself that you're not alone—and to give you some good advice. The most important times to call on your allies are these: first thing in the morning, before you open your eyes; around the middle of the day to help you get your bearings and remember who you are; and last thing at night, after you turn out the lights. For your nighttime gathering, try to imagine your allies involved in some amiable discussion that makes you happy. It's relaxing and healthy for your body if you fall asleep that way. In just a moment I'll give you more instructions about useful conversations to imagine in your nighttime gathering, but first I want to alert you to one very important time you should gather your allies, and this one is unscheduled.

You should always gather your allies whenever you feel like an orphan.

Whenever something happens to make you feel alone or unsure, whenever you start worrying that your dreams are wrong or you are foolish for wanting them, that's your cue to call on your allies. Dreams are delicate in the beginning. They're built on nothing but hope and vision. Until they develop some momentum it's very easy for dreams to crash and burn. Feelings of isolation make them even more precarious.

That's when you start to feel hurt, even though you may not realize it.

At such times, you might try to shake off these feelings by talking yourself out of them. But self-talk isn't enough to soothe that ache in your heart that comes when you feel so alone. The resources to help you get your balance back are inside you, but it's hard to get access to them by simply telling yourself to feel better. That only reinforces the isolation and confirms that you have no one to talk to but yourself. Imagining allies can usually jump the gap by pulling memories of being taken care of from sometime in our childhood.

You could argue that imagining your allies is just another way of talking to yourself, but you'll find that it's far richer and more colorful. Because minds are nosy and curious, fascinated by what is new, interested in people and stories, your mind will cooperate with you more easily if you provide it with drama and dialogue.

So, instead of praising yourself let your allies praise you and instead of just talking to yourself, ask your allies for advice. It's more dramatic, it's a lot more fun, and it gives you a few moments of feeling like the favorite child instead of an orphan.

Exercise 6: Log Your First Meetings With Your Allies

For the next three or four days, remind yourself to make contact with a few of your allies each morning before getting out of bed, at least once in the middle of the day and each night before going to sleep. If they give you messages, write them on 3 × 5 cards for your memory deck and put a paper clip on them so you'll remember to look at those cards later that day.

Is this program getting hard? Then you're doing it wrong.

Lots of us, like good little children, brace ourselves to do everything as if it were very hard homework. But I want you to avoid at all costs putting meetings with your allies on your list of hard things you ought to do, like sit-ups. *Meetings with your allies belong in the part of your brain devoted to good times and happy fantasies.* That way you'll welcome them easily. Soon, you'll become accustomed to remembering you're somebody who belongs. It's like vitamins for your soul.

If you slip up and forget to call meetings three times a day, don't worry about a thing. It takes only a handful of pleasant encounters to get you used to the notion that you are not alone and to lay tracks in your memory. After a while it will become automatic. Getting to that state doesn't take a lot of hard, consistent work, so don't bother to get rigorous when you practice gathering your allies.

As a matter of fact, I have some ideas about consistency that might surprise you.

Most of us are trained to believe that only persistence and regularity will accomplish anything. That may be true for some things but far fewer than you might imagine. As you read this book, you'll see that most of the exercises in it are short-term, to be done only when you have time. I am very cautious of attempts we make to be consistent, to do anything every day, like clockwork. First of all, it's simply too hard to be consistent. If it weren't, everybody would be. More importantly, trying to be sets you up to fail.

Programs that want you to write every day—or do anything every day—mean well, but I just don't think the expectation is realistic. No matter how long you manage to do any regimen, eventually you stop. Consistency just isn't natural for most of us. I have a friend who did a kind of meditation every morning for three weeks and got a great benefit from it, but feels vaguely ashamed for not keeping it up.

"Did you seriously expect to meditate every single morning for the rest of your life?" I asked.

"It sounds pretty extreme when you say it that way," he answered, "but I still feel like a failure."

Remember, *whenever too many people fail a requirement, there's nothing wrong with them, there's something wrong with the requirement.*

I want to create a program here built on the natural rhythms of real people. Trying to impose some kind of rigid behavior change on yourself is a bit reckless, because the obvious truth is that all the facts are never in. For as long as I can remember I've watched absolute convictions crumble and reassemble as their opposites. I wonder how many people are walking around today with bad backs because they were taught to do sit-ups and leg lifts with their knees locked and their legs straight. I wonder how many people have high cholesterol because for decades we were told to eat as much meat and as few carbohydrates as possible. Breast feeding was considered unsanitary and unscientific by many Americans in the 1930s! Who knows what treasured belief will be the next to crumble?

These kinds of changes should make all of us a bit cautious about taking a new belief so much to heart that we force ourselves into radical changes. Sometimes a bit of inconsistency will prevent you from doing yourself real harm. The old advice of "moderation in all things" applies to self-improvement as much as to self-indulgence. I sometimes think most of our beliefs about what is good for us are based more on leftover religious beliefs from our puritanical roots than on a real assessment of the job to be done. Somewhere behind all the instructions to do something every day is the notion that we must try very hard to be good or we'll naturally slip into badness. As if forgetting to pray every day would make you forget there's a God.

And I advise a big dose of skepticism for any self-improvement program that holds up as models of success the multimillionaires in our history who were supposed to be admirable because they let absolutely nothing stand in their way. A closer look at these industrialists shows us men who were both obsessive and without conscience. Should we really feel like failures if we're not like them?

It's time to accept the truth that the human mind and human endeavor are not built up by daily application. *The mind does not build like a bicep.* We don't learn difficult concepts, for example, by studying them an hour a day, we learn them by studying until we "get it"—and then stopping for a while to let the ideas settle.

Farmers don't plant fields or bring in the hay by the book, they watch the weather. To teach an animal to trust you, for example, you do not treat it well every morning at ten o'clock. You just treat it well whenever you see it. To make a plant grow you don't water it every day, you water it when it gets dry. Creative ideas can't be forced either; they have a life of their own. Studies show that many of the most remarkable ideas came when the thinker was doing something completely unrelated. So have some respect for your own rhythms.

As Ralph Waldo Emerson said, "A foolish consistency is the hobgoblin of little minds." So, be prepared for inconsistency in the exercises coming up in the next chapters. Some chapters—like this one—will require only that you think about something a few times. Others will have you writing like a demon on dozens of sheets of paper in a whirlwind exercise designed to stir up a hundred memories.

But whatever I ask you to do in this program, my goal is to keep the requirements realistic and allow you to feel that you're doing a good job. That's not coddling. That's good common sense.

Don't forget to date anything you write

Because this program is not rigidly structured, and skipping a few days here and there is perfectly all right, it's important to have another way to give you a sense of structure—just like the rhythm in the background of a song gives the melody a base to steady it.

For you, that structure will be time. Therefore, *always put the date and the time of day on every page and every 3 × 5 card you write on.* I recommend taping a year calendar inside your notebook so you can refer to it easily.

If you put the time and date on every page you write, you'll soon see a pattern emerge. That pattern will reflect the demands of your life and your own natural rhythms. This information is invaluable. Stops and starts that are caused by the events of your life seen over a long period of time will reveal the shape of your lifestyle and the rise and fall of your energy levels like a seismograph. If you're going to design a life that fits you you need to know how you function naturally.

You'll also be learning some powerful lessons about time itself, how it moves steadily along and the world moves with it, no matter how you feel. That's not a limitation, it's a strength. It's reassuring to understand that you are part of a continuity that exists in nature. After a while you'll come to see that time itself, because it protects you from shapelessness, because it makes you pace yourself, and because it reminds you to keep moving, could very well be one of your greatest allies.

One of the most important messages this ally time will give you is that you don't have forever. For that alone, you owe it a thank you. *But only if it persuades you to keep moving, and not to panic.*

It's going to feel a bit strange at first to work inconsistently like this, but if you take a closer look, there's probably no change at all in the way you *actually* do things, just a radical change from the way you think you *should* do things.

We imagine ourselves to be virtuous when we set standards that we never meet, as long as we feel bad about our failure to meet them! If my instructions seem too slack, too easy, that's because they don't create this illusion of virtue.

There's much to unlearn here. One day you'll listen to your own feelings and know what you should be doing for yourself moment by moment. Don't let anyone tell you something is wrong with that much individuality. I don't know if you can run an entire society or an army this way, but you can and you must go after your dreams with your individuality turned up all the way, or you'll wind up with somebody else's life. That would be a terrible loss to you. And to the world

Back to your allies

Your allies are going to be useful to you in more than one way, and I'd like you to practice a few of these ways as soon as possible. The first night, as I suggested, you should try to imagine your allies engaged in a pleasant or interesting conversation about anything. Just imagine them all talking to each other as you fall asleep. That will get you accustomed to their presence.

The next night, imagine them talking to each other about you, praising you in very specific terms. Don't have them say, "She's wonderful." That's too general. Let them get into details. "She's wonderfully smart," or wonderfully artistic or intuitive or kind. This might make you feel so exhilarated you won't be able to fall asleep. It could just as easily make you feel sad by contrast with reality. Most people don't get much praise in daily life, but we all need it very much. I think receiving praise makes us brave. Down deep we really know our worth, but we don't have easy access to that knowledge. We need to hear praise coming from outside ourselves or we won't remember that we deserve it.

There's one more function that allies fulfill beautifully: they give great advice. So the next night, I want you to try something: ask your allies a tough question. If there's something you've had trouble resolving, imagine them discussing it until you drop off to sleep. In the morning, give yourself a few quiet moments before you jump out of bed to see if you've got an answer.

☜❖ MEMORY DECK ALERT

When you wake up, catch your first thought, write it on a 3 × 5 card. Head it "First thoughts," and add it to your Memory Deck to carry around with you during the day. You'll often find that your first morning thought carries valuable information for you.

Now you've got some terrific additions to your Memory Deck. In addition to giving yourself what you need to best motivate yourself, you've now added a list of very special allies to keep you company on your journey.

This path toward a life you love is starting to look nicer than you expected, isn't it?

LESSON THREE

Understand Your Feelings

"The young man who has not wept is a savage, and the old
man who will not laugh is a fool."

GEORGE SANTAYANA

✦

"By starving emotions we become humorless, rigid and ste-
reotyped; by repressing them we become literal, reformatory
and holier-than-thou; encouraged, they perfume life; discouraged, they poison it."

JOSEPH COLLINS

*Feelings play a special role in the journey toward a life you will
love. They serve as a compass that will guide you toward the right
goals, but they can also gather up into a heavy burden that can
stop you. Because behind everything you do—or avoid doing—are
your feelings. If you find you're often stopping yourself, or if you
just don't know what direction to take or what you really want, all
you have to do is listen to—and understand—your feelings.*

*They're talking to you and they know what you need. Are they
always right? Not always. Sometimes they mistake the present for
the past. At those times, the fear or anger or hurt you feel belong
somewhere else. But there's a way to send feelings about the past
back to where they belong and see the present with fresh eyes.*

The problem is, you can't use reason or logic to do it.

Reason and logic are latecomers to human development. Feelings have been with us longer and remain far more powerful. Happiness and hurt, fear and anger, have all been put there by nature to protect us and keep our species alive. They're in operation every moment of every day, driving us to act—or to avoid action. The expectation of pleasure or safety draws us closer to food, love, shelter. And the apprehension of pain or danger pushes us away from snarling animals and unfamiliar territory.

For the most part, feelings do an admirable job at keeping us away from danger and sending us toward nourishment and affection. But they become increasingly tangled as we move into more complex areas. Nature sends primitive reactions into more subtle, modern situations, so although our survival is in no real danger, we cringe at the risk of rejection when we ask our boss for a raise; we wince at the thought of telling a parent that we want a career in acting; we give up our dreams rather than feel the guilt of becoming happy when our parents weren't.

Often, we're completely unaware of the feelings at work in our attempts to go after a life we love and we make the mistake of applying logic to these issues. The result is confusion. After all, there's no logical reason to avoid rejection or criticism or happiness. They won't kill you—right?

Tell that to your feelings.

No, you can't ignore your emotions. They're strong and primitive and must be dealt with. Lesson Three will teach you some of their language so you can listen to what they are saying and choose how to react.

Lesson Three:
Understand Your Feelings

That marvelous mind you were born with is packed with amazing, rich stuff. It's crowded with memories and plans, expectations and habits, survival instincts and world views—and talents waiting to sprout. In Lesson Three you'll be going on a research expedition to explore one very important part of your interior world, one that has enormous influence on you: your feelings.

First, let's take a look at what your feelings do for you.

1. *They guide you:* Your feelings are your compass. If you know how to read them, they will direct you toward what you love. And they will react in odd ways every time you start to move in a direction that just isn't right. If you know what you feel, you're protected from the influence of people who may be advising you badly.

2. *They connect you to others:* Your feelings give you a sense of belonging to the human race. You're like everyone around you when you love your children, need security, enjoy a certain amount of adventure; like everyone else, you can be hurt by unkindness or tickled by a good joke. In that sense, there are no strangers.

3. *They distinguish you from others:* While your feelings help you to connect with your fellow humans (for the most part) they also show how distinct you are. Your reactions and your preferences are uniquely yours, and they make themselves known by feelings. One person may love cats and

hate baseball, fear swimming and enjoy mountain climbing—but you may be exactly the opposite. Because we're all so different, you have to listen carefully to others and try to know their reactions and preferences before you advise them. And you always have to be prepared for people who don't listen to you carefully, and who affectionately try to steer you in a direction that *they* would love. As long as you know what you're feeling, you won't make the mistake of accidentally living your life according to someone else's vision. As Confucius says, "The wise person listens to everyone and thanks them for their opinion. Then he sends them away and does what he thinks best."

4. *They make you intuitive:* When you know what you feel, you know what others are feeling, too. You don't have to be psychic, just in touch with your own feelings. Animals and babies react instinctively to the feelings of others, because they're emotionally wide open. When you're in touch with your own feelings you also have a sense of what's going on behind people's facades. Anytime you suspect someone isn't being honest, for example, that's your instinct speaking through your feelings, and most of the time it's on the mark. Of course, you always want to back feelings up with reason whenever possible, but never ignore a strong hunch.

When you're out of touch with your feelings, you don't understand other people very well and that's inherently scary. Filmmakers know this: when they want to scare you, they design monsters or creatures from another species or crazy humans whose feelings you can't possibly identify with.

5. *They signal problems:* Your feelings call out when you need to take care of yourself. Unhappiness or hurt draws your attention to a problem that needs fixing, just like

physical pain sends you to a doctor. Uneasiness tells you be careful, happiness shows you've done the right thing. Your feelings give you instant feedback about the world, by sending off alarms when you're in danger and calming down when it's past.

6. *Being aware of them makes you patient with yourself and others:* When you understand and admit all your feelings you realize that perfection is impossible. If you know what it's like to be afraid of heights or dogs, or you recognize you have a jealous streak you're not too crazy about, you're forced to acknowledge that humans are not perfect. It's good to be tolerant of imperfection just because it's always a good idea to accept reality—even if you're trying to change it.

Why don't we know what we're feeling?

One of the biggest problems in our culture is that we think so many feelings are unacceptable. If you're a politician, you only want to be serious and friendly. If you're a good parent, you only want to feel kind and loving. If you're trying to be a tough guy, you avoid friendly or kind feelings and try to be threatening and aggressive.

Now, if you were only faking, if you knew what you were feeling but decided to keep your true feelings a secret, it wouldn't create such a big a problem for you. But in fact, most of us don't want to fake it; we sincerely want to disown our "unacceptable" feelings. We say, "I'm not afraid, I'm not angry, I'm not disappointed," until we don't know what we're feeling at all. *That's* a problem.

I'd like to change your attitude about feelings. I'm hoping that when you know what your feelings are, you'll be more interested in listening to what they're saying than trying to change them. Instead of thinking your feelings are dangerous, you'll look on them as friends.

Naming your feelings

Let's take a general overview of our emotions. One useful way to get a sense of the terrain is to sort our feelings into a few major categories.

Happiness

One group of feelings goes under this lovely name, happiness. The happiness group includes total exhilaration of course, but it also includes a comfortable calm, or a sense—easy to overlook—that nothing's missing. Anytime something makes you laugh you're happy, if only for the moment you're laughing. When you look forward to seeing someone or like hearing someone's voice on the phone, you're happy. Don't forget to pay attention to small moments of happiness. Even on a bad day, you can usually find quite a few of them.

Fear

Fear happens when your system senses danger, real or imagined. The degree of perceived danger usually determines how much fear you'll experience. You don't have to be in a screaming panic, running away from a hungry lion to feel fear. It comes in very mild forms as well. If, for example, you are feeling a little blank and not as comfortable as you'd like to be, you're probably experiencing some level of fear. As a matter of fact, one of the characteristics of fear is that your feelings can freeze; you feel numb, as if you don't have any feelings at all. When the adrenaline that causes fear shoots into your system, your behavior can become unpredictable and unreliable. You might run out the door and forget all your important papers or feel rushed when there's plenty of time, or think you're supposed to be somewhere doing something else. Those side effects are actually misplaced jolts of alarm. You feel scared but you're not sure why.

Have you ever had to stand up and deliver a speech? Or been in a terrifying near-miss auto accident? Did you notice how time seemed to slow down and one part of you split off to watch and listen to the other? That was adrenaline shooting into your system, trying to give you the time and distance to get yourself out of trouble.

Fear can also take the form of uneasiness, apprehension, or dread. Like all forms of fear, these feelings come from a sense that danger is hovering nearby, about to happen.

Pain

When I talk about pain I don't mean physical pain, just painful emotions. Pain runs the spectrum from agony right down to wistfulness. Even nostalgia is bittersweet, with a touch of sorrow in it. Feeling what people call "moved," or "touched," means experiencing a combination of sweetness and pain. Then, of course, there are the hurt feelings from someone being unkind, and the hurt of missing people you love. Anything you register as loss always causes some pain, even if it's a small amount.

Pain presents a special problem, because the body can't distinguish between emotional and physical pain. It reads them both as equally dangerous. As a result we often cover pain with fear: we go blank or feel anxious when we should be feeling hurt. If you can find the painful feeling and express it, it will melt anxiety like hot water melts ice and get you back in touch with your real feeling.

Anger

And then there's anger—a complex and, in many cultures, unacceptable feeling. Like other feelings, anger shows itself in different ways. There's the kind of rage that makes you want to hit a punching bag or holler at the top of your lungs, but there is also irritation, or impatience, or frustration. When you feel combative or stubborn, when you want to tease someone in an unkind way— no matter how mild the feeling behind it, it's a form of anger. Sometimes when you're bored with something it can mean you're feeling a little angry at it and don't want to be interested. When you're forced to reject someone because they won't go away, or you feel that someone is making you feel guilty, you often experience some anger as well.

But anger is rarely pure. Often you're only angry on the surface while right underneath it you're very hurt. Sometimes you're angry because you're frightened and you either resent the person who's frightening you or you choose to feel angry because it makes you feel stronger. But occasionally anger is nothing but anger without any pain or fear in it at all. At that point, you could call it "identity anger," the kind that says "I exist. I count. And I've had enough of this!"

Miscellaneous

A couple of feelings don't fit easily into any of the previous categories. Some of them are hybrids, for instance, jealousy— which is often a combination of rage and pain. Guilt is also a hybrid; painful regret mixed with anger—justified or not—at the person who is stimulating your guilt. Embarrassment is often a mixture of pleasure and shame. Indecision looks uncomfortable but is a harbor of safety from the critical voice of perfectionism. And humiliation is pain infused with helpless rage.

Some of our more complex feelings are cover-ups, for example when you feel guilty for something you had no influence over at all. To choose guilt when you had no power to change things is a way of avoiding the more painful and frightening feeling that you are truly helpless.

But guilt isn't all bad by any means. "Good guilt" is a civilizing feeling. It's pain and shame at having hurt someone who didn't deserve it, and the discomfort of this feeling can push you to make amends and behave differently in the future.

A word about bliss

A life you love is going to make you happier, without question, but I'm not trying to lead you to bliss. In the first place, I wouldn't know how. In the second place, I'm very suspicious of the desire for bliss. This is earth. Heaven comes later. On earth you're not supposed to float around beaming at everyone. You're supposed to live your life, fight your fights and laugh and cry. If we were meant to live in heaven, we wouldn't have been born onto the earth.

I'm not teaching serenity, either. If you want to be calm, take long naps and do only familiar things. If you want all your anxiety to go away, eat lots of chocolate or drink lots of beer and spend your days changing channels. It works. You might become as serene as the Buddha himself.

But it's boring and not much fun.

Fun is going after what you want and meeting new people and making discoveries and fashioning things never seen before and learning things you didn't know. That's exciting. And excitement is half joy and half fear—that's the way it is. It's like skiing or diving into a pool—a little scary but lots of fun.

Problem feelings

Your problem feelings will stop you from going after a life you love more often than any forces outside you. Too much fear or anger or misplaced feelings of inadequacy will hold you back when you want to change your life. That's what being "stuck" is usually about: problem feelings that won't change. Feelings are supposed to keep changing, like the weather, and a pattern that won't move causes emotional floods or drought. So problem feelings have to be dealt with in a special way and I'm going to give you some suggestions later in this chapter.

But first you have to understand your own responses, your personal emotional pattern. In just a few moments, you're going to begin your own scientific data collection. You're going to watch the subject—you—walk through her life, and take notes. The first step, just like the first step in any research expedition, is to watch the action and record your observations. You must collect data just as you find it. If you see anger, you can't change it to sweetness and light. If you haven't studied your feelings in this objective way before, you're in for a treat; the next few days will wake you up and make you feel remarkably alive.

But you're sure to run across some strong feelings that you can't quite figure out, so you need a process to help you understand what they are. These strong, uncomfortable feelings usually come up when there's something you should do and you just don't want to. You should confront someone or ask for a favor, but you just hate the idea of doing it. You know these feelings don't make sense because they're out of all proportion to the situation. You need to test them so you can identify them.

The best test I know of for revealing a hidden feeling is to put a little imaginary pressure on it. That is, imagine you're actually doing what you hate to do. That will often push the real feelings to the surface where you can see them.

A man named Bill came to see me for career counseling. He was a skilled engineer with a great work history who'd been laid off when his company merged with another. He knew a lot of people in the business and had a good reputation, so he should have been networking like crazy, but he simply couldn't stand to ask for favors.

"I can't call anyone I know. I can't pick up the phone," he said. "Every time I try, I feel this mass of discomfort and just can't do it."

"What if some force made you carry through even though you didn't want to? What would you feel if you heard a voice on the other end of the line and you asked for a favor?" I asked.

"Like I'm begging," he said. "And I hate it."

"What would you know about begging?" I asked.

"I don't really know."

"Ever have this feeling as a kid?"

He remembered right away. "Yes! My father would never pay attention to me. Never. And I was dying for attention from him. It felt so humiliating."

There was the source of the discomfort. Humiliation. The wonderful thing about finding the hidden feeling is that you stop being stuck and get into motion again. Once free, feelings know exactly how to process themselves.

Tears came into Bill's eyes and he looked at the floor for a long time, remembering those painful moments. I know how feelings can magically transform themselves when you simply express them, so I let him stay silent as long as he wanted. When he seemed to be finished with the hurt feelings, I asked him to imagine picking up the phone and asking for help again.

"Does it still feel like begging?"

"No!" he said, a bit surprised. "It just feels like asking, like when I ask my wife or daughter for something. Simpler. Not painful and complicated like it was before."

What had happened? Knowing the source of his feeling and allowing himself to express the hurt from his childhood had pulled the past out of the present. Now he could see what was really going on instead of clouding it with childhood pain. And all this was done because we *looked* for the real feeling instead of trying to *change* it.

Getting in touch with heavy, loaded feelings from the past and allowing yourself to express them—is far more useful than trying to reason yourself out of them. Every time Bill lectured and scolded himself, or tried to reason with himself for not making his phone calls he got nowhere. That's because no matter how right reason and logic may be they aren't usually strong enough to change your feelings.

A woman named Emily came to see me recently. She was in a sales training program at her company but was having a hard time with face-to-face selling.

"I just hate to make people do something they don't want to do, or to manipulate and pressure them into signing on the dotted line. I feel so terrible when we do our motivational sales meetings, cheering and shouting to give ourselves energy and courage. It makes me feel like a fake. A loser."

"Why?" I asked.

"I'm afraid I'm just a bad salesperson. I'm too weak to get what I want from people. I care more about them than myself. I've been told that I don't have the self-esteem to sell."

I was shocked. To show her what she was really feeling, I described an experiment I'd read about many years ago. It was done with children in a first grade class to find out if natural salesmanship showed up in childhood. Each child was given six bad-tasting crackers and the rules were that if you couldn't get someone else to eat the crackers, you had to eat them yourself. Although the pressure to influence others was very clear, most of the children couldn't bring themselves to "sell" the crackers. One would ask his neighbor if she'd eat his crackers, but when she refused he understood perfectly. He wouldn't have done it either. But a few children really knew how to sell. They wheedled, begged, pretended to cry, threatened, made false promises—anything to get the other kids to eat their crackers. They were the successes.

The conclusion? The most successful salespeople were kids with no empathy. The winners had no ability to identify with other people's feelings, so they didn't care how the "buyer" felt.

"How do you like that?" I said. "Want to be someone with no empathy?"

"Never!" she said, feeling shocked at the results of the experiment and a lot better about herself. She finally got the picture of who she was. Caring about other people's feelings was her gift. She had a talent for understanding people and a heartfelt desire to help them; and helping people is an essential element of the good life for people like Emily.

As for her self-esteem, I thought hers was very high. "You couldn't bring yourself to go against what you believed in," I told her. "That's the greatest sign of self-respect you can have!"

Emily went on to become a very successful salesperson because she found out what the best salespeople know: repeat business is built on trust. "I spend a lot of time researching a product, and if it won't really help people, it's out. But if it will, I sell it with all my heart." She passed up a lot of chances for quick money, but with the products she chose, she ranked in her company's top ten salespeople nationwide for four years running.

So you can usually trust your feelings if you follow them to their source, but be prepared for some puzzles. Just turn the puzzling feelings over and look at them carefully. Use some of the techniques that Bill and Emily used, and you'll often find out what's hiding right underneath the surface. As you can see, that knowledge can make all the difference in the world to you.

All right, let's begin your research project by experimenting on the feelings of this interesting creature you live with: yourself.

Exercise 1: Emotions Checklist

Below is a list of every feeling I can think of. If you find that I've overlooked anything—and I hope you do—add it to the list. Look it over.

happy
scared
hurt
angry
calm
watchful
bored
turned off
comfortable
easy
tickled
playful
interested
expectant
hopeful
worried
dreading
guilty
relieved
hurried
irritable
nervous

restless

fussy

uneasy

embarrassed

disappointed

sad

your additions

Okay, scientist, here's how to start tracking yourself.

●◇ MEMORY DECK ALERT

Copy the list above onto both sides of a 3 × 5 card in your Memory Deck—with the heading "Emotions," and carry it around for three days. You could well be adding new feelings to the list for the next few days, so you might need extra blank cards. Once the list is copied, here's what you do.

Each time you're aware of having a feeling, scan the list and place a small check after the word that describes it. A lot of checks after "watchful," and very few after "playful," for example, can tell you a lot about yourself. If that's a typical pattern of yours, that is if you find yourself with lots of checks after "watchful" and very few after "playful" day after day, it's very revealing. Have you been that way since childhood, or did this pattern start after some event a few years ago? Is your whole family this way? Did they teach that kind of behavior? Whatever you find out about yourself is valuable. I promise you'll need it sooner or later.

If, on the other hand, this pattern is not typical, if it only shows up for a short time, it's being triggered by something you may not have been aware of. Whenever your typical pattern changes, you can be sure that something else is going on, and you need to do some searching to bring it to light. You might find that a new element in your life—a new relationship, a new kind of work, a change in the weather or your body chemistry—is affecting you more than you realized. Again, that's valuable information for you.

What if you find yourself unable to identify what you're feeling? Just do your best to describe it and add it to the list no matter how odd it looks. If you find yourself writing descriptions like "jittery and cranky," or "weird, empty, like someone just left" that's fine. What matters is that every time you notice yourself feeling that way again, place a check after it.

Carry this Memory Card wherever you go for three days (more, if you like) and do your best to be alert to any feelings you have. At first, you're sure to forget to pay attention, but that will soon change and you'll find it much easier to notice your feelings. As a matter of fact, for a little while you're probably going to go a bit overboard because it's such an exciting revelation to register so much internal action for the first time. Just remember to pay attention to traffic and try not to bore people too much by talking about your discoveries. Once you get used to feeling emotionally awake, you'll become less preoccupied with yourself. *But your feelings will never totally disappear from your awareness again.* Anytime you want to, you'll be able to dip into your interior world and know what's going on.

So keep your pencil and your Memory Card ready for the next few days. Try taking them to a family gathering and see what you feel after a brother or sister or parent speaks to you. Try making checks while you're watching a movie or directly before and after a job interview. Before long, you won't need the pencil or the card. Just a few days of doing this exercise will make you permanently more aware of your feelings.

Exercise 2: Remembrance of Emotions Past

Now take another look at that list of feelings you just wrote down and let your eyes fall on any one of the words on the list. Then close your eyes and see if any memory comes back to you. For example when I looked at the word "dreading," I flashed back on my Spanish class in junior high and how I sat in dread that the teacher would call on me. Every time she called on someone and it wasn't me, I felt relief. Then I felt dread at the next question. When she finally called on me, I felt as if I were in front of a firing squad. My brain went blank and I could hear my mouth saying the answer—the wrong answer probably—as though it were someone else speaking. That was fear, pure and simple.

So I found out a lot about myself from just looking at the word "dreading." Try it out for yourself. And not just once. Anytime you have a few moments, just glance at the list of feelings and let your mind fly into the past. Over time, this exercise will start recovering your emotional history for you. *You'll be creating an autobiography every time you recover the memory of an emotional scene in your life—and a fascinating one at that.* If you feel like writing these scenes down in your notebook, by all means do so. I happen to believe that everyone should write their autobiography. I wish my great grandparents had written theirs, and your grandkids will be thrilled if you write yours. However, if you decide not to, don't worry; you'll never forget an emotional flashback even if you don't write it down.

These exercises will wake you up to a rich inner life. If you never thought much about your emotions before, be prepared to feel as if you have a technicolor epic film going on inside you. You should enjoy this very much, but if it becomes too intense let it rest for a while. Put the feelings card in the back of the deck and carry on as you always have. Peek at it every now and then to see if you're ready to get started again. You'll know.

And then you can go back to these exercises and this "wake up" list.

Once you do you'll be ready to move to the next step of personal research: finding out when and why your feelings show up.

Exercise 3: Log Your Feelings

Now I want you to start writing about your feelings with an eye to what could have triggered them. To do that, you need to keep track of *when* a feeling shows up. Ask yourself, when did I start feeling that? What happened just before that? That kind of thinking will give you insights to why you're having a certain feeling.

So, open your notebook, write today's date and the time of day, and head the page with these words:

"Feelings Log"

Here's your first assignment. For the next few days I want you to pay attention to your feelings and write a description in your notebook of what they were, when they occurred and the circumstances surrounding their appearance, as if it were a ship captain's log. I want you to find out what makes you feel good and what makes you sad, what irritates you, what frightens you, what makes you nervous, what you try to avoid. All you have to do is simply state what happened immediately preceding the feeling: "I stepped outside into the rain and felt happy for no apparent reason." Or "Felt uneasy. Just remembered the report that's due tomorrow." Period.

Notice that this is not a feelings *journal.* In a feelings journal you might write something like: "I feel bad about Mary's success, and I'm so ashamed of that. She's always been so nice to me. It isn't that I want her to fail. . . ." Et cetera.

In a log, however, you write like a ship's captain, without editorializing: "Mary told us about her good luck. I felt a pang of bad feeling." End of report.

You need to look at your emotions with the same disinterested respect you'd have if you were studying a hurricane or an amoeba. We all have the habit of trying to hide our feelings from ourselves. We automatically deny uncomfortable feelings and try to turn them into comfortable ones. It's not easy to catch yourself doing that.

And if the event that triggered the feelings seems too small to have mattered, your active brain is going to go looking for something fancier and overlook the right event, so this project could be a bit difficult at first. But hang on; it will get easier. The previous two exercises have warmed you up and over the course of a few days, you'll find yourself becoming a real student of your own feelings.

Let me tell you something that might surprise you: simply logging your feelings in this way will do more in making you accept yourself—and respect yourself—than a hundred affirmations saying "My feelings are all right," or "I am a good person." *The very act of noting something means you accept it.* Look at any scientist's log, any captain's log, and you'll see an acceptance and respect for reality, loud and clear.

What if you only want to relate to your good feelings?

"I only want to feel positive."

"Negativity is terrible. I want no part of it."

"I just want to be happy and find my passion."

Is that you? Well, all I can say is, "Good luck."

We can all remember a time when we felt positive, bold, sure of ourselves—when we were able to do hard projects as though they were easy. But I also remember times I felt rotten for weeks, and just couldn't get rolling. Is there anything we can do to get through the bad feelings fast so we can return to the good ones?

There is a way, but squashing your feelings and trying to replace them with good thoughts won't do it.

To work with feelings, you must use feelings.

If you're feeling hurt, you probably need to cry. If you're scared, you might need to scramble for safety. If you're angry, you might need to do some squawking about the injustice in your life. That's the way we're born. And though we're trained to control these feelings in public, and to think before we act on them— wisely taught, incidentally—that doesn't mean that we should make this kind of control a habit in our personal lives.

My advice? If you're not alone, don't swallow your feelings, simply postpone them for a few moments, then go somewhere private and express them. Cry, tremble, shake your fists and curse your enemies. Do whatever the feeling seems to want you to do.

Yes, that's what I said: groan or heave heartbreaking sighs in the bathroom. Snarl and punch your palm in the coat closet. Shiver and admit you're scared to death. I know it sounds dopey, but just a few minutes of expressing your feelings will radically lower their intensity and give them a chance to transform themselves, the natural way. The way a thundershower clears away dark clouds.

Unexpressed feelings are toxic. *That's why nature gave us the tools of expression—to discharge the toxins that have built up inside.* As far as I'm concerned, expressing feelings is the only natural way to turn a bad feeling into a good one. Not by saying "I will not feel negative," but by letting a negative feeling have its moment of release so it can lighten up and change by itself.

You can try to bluff yourself, of course, and sometimes there's nothing else to do. It's called "whistling in the dark," meaning that you're pretending not to be afraid when you're in a dark tunnel. If you have no other options, by all means whistle. But when you're alone, drop the tough facade and let the fear and hurt and anger burst out or you'll have to carry them around with you for days, weeks, or longer until they leak into scenes of your life where they don't belong and wreak havoc.

So, although I know it's not very popular these days to say so, over the long haul, trying to pretend you feel better than you do doesn't work. I see no evidence that you can change how you feel simply by repeating a slogan over and over. To me, the signs they put up in corporations about "Excellence" and "Integrity" represent some oversimplified form of primitive magic: say the word often enough and you will evoke the spirit. But repeating slogans doesn't create real change. Your internal defense machinery can run circles around self-hypnosis, and the mind is so creative it eventually resents the dullness of repetition.

As far as I'm concerned, there's only one affirmation that works.

"I yam what I yam," or Popeye to the rescue.

If you think this affirmation is too modest or not good enough, take a look at Popeye's behavior in the old animated cartoons on TV. Here is a character who knows how to live and love, doesn't look for trouble but handles it when it comes to meet him. Personally, I think he qualifies as an Ally.

Try saying Popeye's affirmation and see how it feels. "I yam what I yam, and that's all that I yam." It's a wonderful corrective to the myth of infinite perfectability that exhausts us all. It looks modest, but this affirmation is a bit cocky. I find it refreshing. It's got a subtext that says "I am what I am. Take it or leave it."

> **•← MEMORY DECK ALERT**
>
> If you like Popeye's affirmation as much as I do, write it on a card for your Memory Deck. That way you'll stumble on it at unexpected times and it will get you back on course, enjoying who you are instead of always trying to improve yourself.

The Joy of Negativity

Whenever I try to repeat an affirmation over and over (even Popeye's!) my subconscious rebels and starts handing me irritated responses, like "Shutup already," or "Every day in every way I'm getting fatter and fatter."

But those responses make me smile: apparently something inside me finds that negativity is fun. Before you judge a feeling, remember to simply note it just as a good scientist would, and look to see if there's a good reason for it.

Well, in this case, I think there is a reason. Inside every one of us is a defiant brat that doesn't always feel like doing the right thing. If we're supposed to be saying affirmations, we irreverently create satires.

I don't think rebelliousness is a bad sign. Irreverence is a declaration of independence and it announces that you have a mind of your own. You may have been taught to consider it a failure that you haven't stuck with your affirmations, but I consider it a triumph for your freedom-loving spirit. My advice? Call them "Negations" and have some fun with them. Here's how.

Exercise 4: The Negativity T-Shirt Company

Pretend you have started your own business as a T-shirt designer, and you've decided that nothing will sell as well as "Negations." Open your journal to a blank sheet and draw ten outlines of T-shirts about two inches high, like this.

Leave the T-shirts blank and the pages open as you think about things that irritate you. The moment you come up with something, walk over to the page and write a "Negation" on one of the T-shirts.

I've gotten photos in the mail of people wearing T-shirts they had written on with marking pens! Here are some of the memorable "negations" people have come up with.

"Don't even think about hugging me."

"I want to be the favorite!"

"It's everybody else's fault but I always get blamed."

"I believe I'm tall."

"What does 'deserve' mean?"

"I need an apartment!"

"Don't feed me."

"I feel great. Do you hate me for that?"

"Hi! I'm an idiot!"

"I'd give it all up to be the best looking human in the world. (Am I shallow?)"

"Where's my mom?"

"Don't let the bastards get you down."

As you can see, some of the negations were actually positive, but they were fresh and new, not tired and corny. Change them often and they'll always make you feel a lot better because *it always does you good to make your own statement.* On the front of a T-shirt it's like an advertisement for your inner self. It's your own way of saying "I yam what I yam. Take it or leave it."

I have yet to meet the person who doesn't enjoy coming up with really awful negations. When I do this exercise in my workshops, the participants write paper signs and pin them to their shirts. At any time, they can change their signs if their mood changes. This notion of making a momentary statement and wearing it as an item of clothing strikes me as inspired.

But even if you're only drawing T-shirts in your journal, designing them still creates an opportunity to release a backed-up load of negativity and make you smile at the same time. So prepare your drawings of blank negativity T-shirts and wait for the spirit to grab you, then fill them in. My only rule is that you try to write your statements from real feelings instead of just trying to be witty.

There's one more feeling I want to discuss. It stands out in a category of its own and I've it saved for last because it has a special relation to going after a life you love. It's called "passion."

Feeling Passion

People talk a lot about passion, but not many people claim to have it. You don't usually experience it in your work; you just hope you will someday.

Personally, I think "passion" is an intimidating word. It's not much like "anger" or "happiness," or other feelings I've mentioned. It's more like "glamour," or "heroism," traits you see in other people but rarely experience yourself.

Lots of people come to see me for counseling because they haven't found their passion, and when I find out what they mean I can see why they're lost. They seem to think that to be happy they must be driven—even obsessed—by their chosen work. But love is not necessarily passion. In fact, I'm willing to say that the best kind of love probably isn't passion. Think about someone you love wholeheartedly—your spouse or your mom, your child or your dog or your best friend—and see if you call that passion. I don't. Passion is hot stuff, it excludes everything else, and it burns out fast. I don't think it's all it's cracked up to be.

I know people who have achieved exactly the kind of lives they want. They paint or travel or teach or write and they enjoy every minute of it. I include myself among them. We feel very fortunate to be able to spend most of our time doing work we love. But not one of us would describe ourselves as being in a state of high passion about our work. We might occasionally say that we feel passionate about undoing some terrible wrong, or obsessed by a project or a person, but I know of no one who actually looks forward to such a feeling.

I hate to disappoint you, but maybe I can save you some time if I tell you passion could be the wrong emotional measuring stick when you're looking for a good life. In my experience with my own life and the lives of my clients, I've found that the need for passion comes from an aching emptiness in the heart. That emptiness seems so huge that we incorrectly assume it can only be filled by a giant passion. But that's not so.

When you start doing the work you were born to do, you don't feel passion. What you feel is that nothing is missing. One person after another, on finding their life's work has said to me, "It was like putting on a comfortable old shoe," "I sighed with relief and relaxed," or "I knew I was finally doing the right thing." Imagine contentment combined with lots of steady energy for work that is absorbing.

To me, that beats passion every time.

Good going. You've completed Lesson Three.

Look at what you've done. You've learned the names of your feelings and paid attention to them as they appeared inside you. You've recovered feelings from your past and maybe even started an autobiography. You've logged your feelings, and possibly spotted some emotional triggers. You've found that you don't have to be afraid of any of your feelings, not even negative ones. And if you thought you were missing something—like passion—I hope you don't think that anymore.

You're not missing anything at all. You're a complete and superb emotional package. You were born that way. All that was needed was a good look at your rich and colorful interior so you'd understand what the disturbances were all about, and of course, to find out what makes you happy. You'll be needing this knowledge as we proceed with the upcoming lessons but for now, just enjoy the information.

LESSON FOUR

Clear the Decks for Action

"Clutter, a clotted mass; as a verb, it is a variant of 'clotter,' to run into clots. Clutter also meant confusion, a confused heap, turmoil, din; by association with 'clatter,' from 'kloter,' a rattle."

A CONCISE ETYMOLOGICAL DICTIONARY OF THE ENGLISH LANGUAGE, WALTER W. SKEAT

✦

"Disorder and procrastination help avoid boredom; one never has the feeling that there is nothing important to do."

ANONYMOUS

You can't create a life you love when your present life is hopelessly crowded with obligations. You've got to make room for a wish to come true. So Lesson Four is dedicated to teaching you how to clear the decks for action.

First, let's establish my credentials for discussing clutter. One, I'm a hopeless pack rat for anything sentimental. Two, I have dozens of projects going on at the same time and others that I plan to get to very soon. And three, I love to create systems for organizing my complicated life, but I usually change them in the middle and forget what I was doing.

All the same, I've learned how to make room for a project. And a wish.

Here are some of my discoveries:

Clutter is the almost inevitable residue of creative people. We love the sense of potential that hovers around a pile of magazines, a stack of books, a box of random items. The thought that we could find information, organize things, start a project—just as soon as there's time, of course—makes it hard to get rid of anything. In fact, creative people usually add to the clutter every day with new purchases, new found objects, and stuff that comes in the mail that we think we'll have some creative use for one day.

The problem is that clutter doesn't create opportunities to do wonderful projects, it stops them. With no extra space or time, with all these overdue projects around the house—magazines to be read, books to be read, projects to be done—the mind has no room to open up new ideas.

Don't expect Lesson Four to give you orders to throw everything out. That doesn't work. We attach to our possessions in complex ways, and fill them with deep meaning. Sending a bulldozer through the house to shove them out the door and into a Dumpster is something we can't bear to do. No, we have to find other ways to deal with our possessions.

But they must be dealt with. *Not so the neighbors and your mom will admire you, far from it. I intend to encourage you to fill up that space and time all over again! But when you do, it will be with something you have chosen, work you will love. You'll be discovering what that work is in the lessons to come. But, like songbirds, your hidden dreams won't come to your home unless you give them a place to perch.*

Lesson Four:
Clear the Decks for Action

Questionnaire

Ask yourself the following questions:

1. Do you have clothes in your closet that haven't fit you for years?
2. Do you own appliances and gadgets you don't use?
3. Do you own anything broken that you intend to fix someday?
4. Do you have all the materials for projects you never find the time to do?
5. Are you planning to have a lawn sale one of these days, but you dread all the work it will take?
6. Do you have unfinished chores to do, papers to sort, cards to send, letters to write?
7. Do you save junk mail and catalogs?
8. Do you get calls from people you don't really want to talk to?
9. Do you have magazines waiting to be read?

If you answered yes to any of these questions you've got a problem. And don't think you're going to solve your problem by just sorting out everything and making big lists. That's a common myth: "One of these days I'll find a place for everything I want to keep, I'll go through every piece of mail and through all those catalogs, I'll just save what I want and toss out the rest, and as soon as I get time I'll get around to answering those letters and phone calls.''

Don't you believe it. You're never going to get that clutter under control and you might be very surprised to find out why. *You haven't accidentally accumulated all that stuff. It's part of an unconscious plan.*

You've created the clutter for a reason.

Clutter: a tribute to indecision

If you think that the chronic accumulation of clutter is nothing more than the problem of a disorderly or overextended person, I have a surprise for you: clutter isn't a problem for you. Clutter *solves* a problem for you.

Clutter in the background gives the illusion that you're surrounded by projects just waiting to be done. It makes you feel that life is full of potential. The things that crowd your corners and shelves and closets may look like junk to other people, but to you every single item represents opportunity. A magazine article could give you information that would change your life. That broken near-antique chair would look beautiful in your living room if only you had the time to get it fixed. It also might be worth serious money. What if you just threw all those things out? It would be such a loss of opportunity. You could be sorry later on.

So why don't you read the magazines or find out where to fix the chair? Because you're too busy? Don't believe it. The fact is, reading that magazine and researching that chair are very far down on your list of priorities, and if you don't believe me, ask yourself a question: what do you do when you have a free hour? The answer is written all over your house. You use that time for anything besides getting rid of clutter. No, being too busy isn't your reason for keeping clutter in your life. Uncomfortable though it may be to have so much unfinished work surrounding you, you keep those magazines and broken antiques because all that potential feels nice.

Now take one more step in your thinking and what you'll find is a tiny but powerful fear of commitment.

Clutter is like a modern sculpture you've assembled all around you, a monument that pays tribute to indecision. With all those projects waiting you can't possibly choose anything important to do. Clutter may be loaded with potential but it kills any chance of setting up an easel and painting or starting your own home business. Not only is there no floor space, there's never any time. After all, you have to take care of all this clutter first, don't you?

Now why would anyone stop themselves from making a commitment to something they might love to do? After all, the people you envy most are those who have done just that. Well, for one thing, you might not know yet what you want to do. And for another, commitment changes your life. That's scary for everybody. You'll be getting all kinds of help for that as you go through these lessons, and by the end of this book, you'll begin to do it.

But first, you have to make room for that wonderful day.

So let's find out what makes clutter so tenacious.

You're a person with a lot to do

Clutter solves the problem of boredom and makes you feel needed, like a busy person with important things to do. Before you laugh, think about it for a moment. Imagine you're in a beautiful room, empty of any furniture but a comfortable chair, and a coffee table with a telephone and a good book resting on it. Nothing else. You've caught up on every single obligation you had, and now everything is spacious and sunny. Now, in your fantasy, you can catch up on all that reading you wanted to do. Doesn't that sound great? You'd love an opportunity like this, wouldn't you?

No, you wouldn't, *or you'd live in a room like that.* You probably couldn't read more than ten minutes in that room before you started to feel uncomfortable. Why? Because a room like that is *completed.* It doesn't need anybody. Sitting there you'd feel as though you were trapped in a photo from a home decorating magazine.

But, throw a pile of newspapers on the floor and a scissors and some file folders, a pen and a notepad—and everything changes. Pile a few unfinished projects along the wall so you know you'll always feel there's something you need to do, and you'll feel better. Guilty, maybe, because you know you probably won't complete these projects. But better.

In your fantasies you imagine that you'd love to have all the clutter gone so you could relax, *but in fact, nobody really wants to relax.* Not for very long, anyway. Everybody needs something to do.

The problem is that everybody needs something *important* to do, and deep in your heart you sense that reading those magazines or repairing that chair isn't it. You should be finding something to do that matters to you, but unconsciously you're settling for the illusion that you're already in demand and already overextended. It's a brilliant avoidance technique your subconscious defense mechanisms have set up for you.

But this is an expensive little illusion you're supporting here. For all the benefits clutter bestows, it costs you a lot in peace of mind. Clutter makes you feel like a failure, because you never get it under control. It makes you feel guilty because you're not trying harder to clear out that stuff. Those feelings of failure and guilt produce a steady background noise, crowding out more useful thinking.

Worst of all, you're playing a dangerous game when you pretend you have a lot to do because that pretense eats your future. Pretending to yourself that you're busier than you are is both a waste of *real* opportunity, and *real* time. After all, you're not busy fixing that chair, you're just busy worrying about it. And the opportunity that might be waiting for you in some unread magazine article doesn't exist if you don't read the article.

Here's the bad news: there is no potential in clutter at all. The hard and shocking truth is that clutter stops you from doing something you'd love. It's a terrible trick you're playing on yourself.

But what about the stuff you really *have* to do? You know, the thank you cards and the taxes and the broken VCR? They have to be taken care of, don't they?

I maintain, as a recovering pack rat, that people like us can't tell the difference between what we *have* to do and what's part of our pretending game. Of course, you have to do your taxes. But you might not have to send out those thank you cards or fix the VCR. You're about to get a lesson in deciding what's important and what's just another fake out, because that's not something you're good at.

If you don't believe me, look around you.

Myth: All I have to do is get organized

Everything in your house calls to you. There isn't an item in your house that isn't talking to you. It's saying "clean me, read me, fold me, finish me, take me to Aunt Jane's house, answer me, write me" "get your messages, return this here, take that there"—it's a din. It may not be possible to simplify a modern life totally, but to go after a dream, you have to get that racket down to a murmur. Usually our first reaction is that we have to get all that stuff organized—but maybe that's not always a good idea. Let me tell you a story.

When I first got my country place there was a nice old barn behind the house, full of stuff: gardening things (pots and seed containers and string etc., etc.), boxes of books, old furniture, lighting fixtures, and tools. A lovely old car was right in the middle of everything, a 1961 Chevy, which the previous owner had always intended to restore.

Every summer, I would go to the country on the weekends, walk into that huge old barn, and spend all of Saturday trying to organize the mess—what should go on shelves, what should be sold or given away, what should be restored. It was an endless job. I'd usually spend Sunday exhausted and guilty that I wasn't still working in the barn.

And then one day, when I was home in the city, the barn burned to the ground—with all its gardening things, and books, and fixtures, and tools, and that lovely old car! My first feeling was one of utter dismay. What a waste. I was stricken, ready to cry.

My second feeling was enormous relief!

There was nothing left to organize. It was gone, along with all the feelings of being overwhelmed by all that stuff, all the frenzy of hopelessly trying to maintain control by organizing it.

Every weekend since then I sit on the porch, look out over the hills for a while, then happily read a book. And now the very obvious truth is right in front of me: there's only one good reason to go to the country. To relax, not to exhaust myself moving things around that I shouldn't own in the first place.

You can extend that lesson to your whole life: for whatever purpose you were put on this planet, it couldn't be to organize clutter.

> ## ☞ MEMORY DECK ALERT:
> ## TRICKS TO CONQUER CLUTTER
>
> In the pages to come, I'll give you a number of tricks I've developed so you won't need a fire to free you from the burden of clutter. Don't forget to write them on a 3 × 5 card for your Memory Deck so you'll have easy access to them in the future.

Here's the first one I want you to write down:

Trick: organize clutter as little as possible

Don't be fooled by the desire to organize your clutter. It's a lifetime job—and a fake one at that. Put your legal and financial papers, your birth certificate, and your insurance policies in one place and tell someone where they are in case they need to find something and you're not there to help them. As for the rest, either get rid of it, or leave it as it is. *For good.* Your photographs are all loose in a couple of big boxes? Fine, you know where to find them if you need them. You can pull out the box and look at your pictures out of order with just as much pleasure as if they were organized by date and glued into albums.

That's the first trick. More are coming. But first you have to find a name for the types of clutter around you because there's a different trick to help you get rid of each kind.

Exercise 1: Name That Clutter

The word "stuff" fits so well because it reminds us of stuffing. All this stuff crowds your thoughts like stuffing in a doll's head; it fills up the available space like stuffing in a turkey. There are many kinds of stuff and each one catches you in a different way. I've isolated seven different kinds most of us have. As you read through the following list, walk around your house and see if you can find the clutter each entry applies to. Then follow the exercises and tricks to deal with that kind of clutter.

1. "It-seemed-like-such-a-good-idea-at-the-time" stuff.

I used to own a few sets of Hungarian language tapes I'd found in a bookstore in the San Francisco airport. I'd been so excited to find them because Hungarian is so different from English and I thought it would be fascinating to understand a bit of it. I tucked them in my bag, boarded the plane and soon was up in the air listening to Hungarian. After three minutes on the headphones, however, I remembered I don't like listening to language tapes. It also occurred to me that I don't need Hungarian for anything, and I'd never be able to learn such a difficult language on my own anyway. So as soon as I got home I put them on my bookshelf and there they stayed for three years; the part of me that remembered how much I dislike listening to language tapes wouldn't pick them up, and the part of me that continued to think it would be fascinating to get a glimpse into Hungarian wouldn't throw them out.

Sound familiar? Look around you. Do you have great old records you always meant to put on audiotape? A box of prints you always intended to frame and hang somewhere? You know in your heart you own things you'll never touch again. What should you do with them? Forget your plans to stage a tag sale in your yard. Unless you're a whiz at such things they're more work than they're worth. Anyway, you shouldn't be handling all this stuff because as soon as you do, your mind starts thinking maybe you should keep it—and that's the last thing you want.

Trick: Call your own bluff

Here's what I want you to do: Walk around your house, notebook and pencil in hand, and note as many of these "seemed-like-a-good-idea-at-the-time" projects as you can: lamps you've intended to fix for years, antique clothes you were going to mend, small cooking appliances for some eating plan you once had. They've become part of the background noise of your life and you don't exactly see them anymore. Having to write them in your notebook will help bring them out of hiding.

Now call your own bluff. Next to each item on your list, write the date you're going to complete the project (sometime soon)—or if you know there is no such date, write "Toss it," and move on to the next group of stuff.

If you have written a date, transfer it to your calendar. *And on that date, you must do it.* You can change the date once or twice for good reasons, but that's all. You have to either put those operas on audiotape and be proud of yourself, or toss them.

Before you close your notebook, however, there's another category of stuff that wants to call your bluff.

2. Stuff that's too expensive to throw out.

This often overlaps with the last category, but the real reason you hang onto this stuff is not because you ever expect to use it but because it cost a lot of money. It's embarrassing to have your eyes continually fall on a box of expensive software you know you'll never use or a great-looking hat you can't bring yourself to wear. Keep your notebook open and write down each item of Type 2 stuff. After each entry put a date by which you promise to use it, or write "Toss it," just as you did earlier.

Is this killing you? Do you feel you absolutely cannot throw this stuff in the trash barrel? I understand perfectly and would never ask you to do anything so wasteful. That's why I have a great trick for getting rid of stuff that's too good for the trash.

Trick: Become a good guy

If you could find someone who really needed your stuff, who would put it to good use and be delighted and grateful to get it, you could turn from an overburdened collector into a public benefactor. For this reason, it's worth spending some time to find an organization where these things might be valued and develop a relationship with it. I found an underfinanced library across town for my books and tapes, and whenever the clutter starts building up in this category, I send it to that library. Now, instead of feeling like a failure for never learning Hungarian, I feel that I might have helped somebody. After all, somebody will want to learn Hungarian one of these days, even if it isn't me.

There's also a hospital that has my opera records in its recreation room. Somebody might be listening to those records and getting a lot of pleasure out of them right now. I sent boxes of beautiful clothes I should never have bought to a women's shelter. I think those women will look far better in them than I would have, and now I don't feel like such a jerk for buying them. Donating to these organizations puts my follies to good use and redeems me. It takes a bit of time to find these places, but you only have to find them once. After that, a phone call will do the job.

3. Invisible stuff.

This is the kind of stuff that grows slowly like moss, so you don't notice until it begins to choke off your breathing space. It's stuff like scratched eyeglasses, broken watches, the battery pack from a camera you no longer own, the wrong color lipstick, worn out sandals you never wear anymore, an outdated calendar with nice pictures of Montana on it, and old ugly pieces of unmatched tableware in the tool box next to rusty wire cutters you will never use. You know this stuff belongs in the trash, but who can take on such a huge project?

Don't fall for the fallacy of the One Big Swoop.

Don't waste a perfectly good Sunday by tying a kerchief around your head, putting on an apron and attacking the junk. I know you think you'll get finished once and for all, but this kind of invisible stuff keeps growing like weeds in your garden. You get rid of them one day and they're back the next. There's simply no way to get rid of it once and for all.

So, what can you do?

Trick: Toss ten things

This trick avoids being a project at all. Instead, you just begin a small, relentless ongoing program to throw out ten things from every room as often as you think of it. If you're combing your hair in front of the bathroom mirror, bring the wastebasket closer, open the medicine chest, and find ten things to throw out while you keep brushing your hair: your cousin's shaving cream, that out-dated prescription you wouldn't dare to touch, those old vitamins. Then, while you're waiting for your coffee to brew, open a kitchen drawer and throw out the broken meat thermometer and the odd butter knife—and eight more things. Then drink your coffee with a smile on your face.

I tend to do this trick in spurts. I forget it for a few months, and then I start up again for a week or so. But that's not a problem. You won't forget to use this trick. You'll remember to come back to it because it's very bracing, like a winter breeze in your face. Just remember a few times each day to throw out ten things and after a while your place will start to look twice its normal size—even light and airy.

4. Stuff that has secondary sentimental value.

Some things have primary sentimental value. They're very important and I don't think you should get rid of them. I'll talk about them later. But often you keep things you wouldn't miss and you never look at, like the pots your kids made in the fifth grade and your school notes from a class you loved. These items have some appeal, but if someone snuck into your home at night and stole only those things, you wouldn't be upset and you know it.

You treat this kind of clutter in the same way as the following kind:

5. Stuff you're keeping for someone else.

You have other stuff around the house that you wish would go away, but which you don't feel you have the right to get rid of. This includes stuff that has sentimental value for someone else like your kids or other relatives: hockey sticks and trophies, trunks of clothes or letters, posters of Elvis Presley. Included in this group are gifts you can't use but are afraid to dump because the nice person who gave it to you might notice. Here's what to do with those two kinds of stuff:

Trick: Pass the buck

Give it back. Find every person who belongs to an item and tell them that you're going to rent out your place and spend a year in Spain, and that your tenant is coming next week to look the place over. Or say that you've decided to sell, and a buyer will be visiting soon. Call your kids and your friends and ask whether they would prefer to pick up their stuff or have you toss it. *Don't give them any other choices.* They've forgotten these things exist, but they'll have a sudden fever of attachment to them, and will soon come to get them. If they don't? Simply name the date you're throwing everything out, remind them a few times (in a bland tone of voice that will scare them), and then dump their stuff on that day. Don't feel guilty. If they really cared, they'd have come.

After a few months if they should notice you're still living in the same place, tell them the deal fell through.

And then there's a very special category of stuff which you should treat differently from any other.

6. Stuff you love and never ever should get rid of.

This is the stuff of primary sentimental value I mentioned before. You own a small number of very special books, letters, journals, photos, and stones or shells from a beach. Every time you look at these things, you feel good. I have a small china statue of two children swinging from a weird little tree and a cardboard box containing every word my children ever wrote. These things stay. If I were crossing the country in a wagon train, I might reduce the number of those items, but I'm not. So, I keep them for company as I walk around my home. They're beautiful, and they remind me that I wasn't born last week, that I have lived a rich life.

No trick is needed for getting rid of this stuff, because it stays. I love it.

Now let's start naming actual chores, the kind that actually has to be done.

7. Stuff that has to be done, but you just can't get started.

What about all those things you know you simply must do, but you're not doing? Finish the back room, go through three years of unfiled tax papers, clean out your garage, pull out a tree stump. Nothing calls to you louder than undone taxes, unorganized bills, unfinished chores. You can't toss those. But here's what you can do. (This is my favorite trick of all.)

Trick: Throw a work party

When my neighbors in the country needed to put in a new milk vat, which requires sawing a section out of the barn and installing a huge steel drum, they set a date and called a lot of neighbors. The wives fried up a batch of chicken while the men sawed and lifted and hammered. Afterwards, everyone sat outside at a picnic table, ate chicken and drank beer. They all had a great time and got the job done. And the crew knows that my neighbor is available whenever they need him in return.

You can do the same with your must-do-but-can't-get-started chores. Call in your friends and create a work party to help you clean your closets or organize your receipts. Feed them, and play some music. They'll give you the courage you need to tackle the job, and it will be done before you start to waver in your resolve.

There you are. Every trick in the book to clear out every kind of clutter and give you space and time and quiet. Get started as soon as you can and before long you'll see major results. And wait until you see what a calm, spacious feeling opens up inside you.

Now, exactly why is it you're cleaning out all this clutter?

Because you need that calm, spacious feeling in order to start the next phase of your life, to make room to do the kind of work you really love.

Now what might that be?

Open your notebook and pick up your pencil. It's time to create some fantasies about a wonderful project or career or home business that could live in that space you're creating. From now on, I'll be giving you lots of opportunities to imagine just what you might enjoy doing, and later you'll get a number of chances to turn fantasies into real goals. It's not decision time yet, so don't get too practical. Just have a lot of fun with your imagination.

Exercise 2: Imagine a Wonderful Project You Could Set up If You Had the Room and the Time

Say you've decided to spend two years traveling around the world. Imagine the space in your home you'll use for that project. Where would you keep the maps and atlases, the phone numbers of the airlines and trains and embassies and travel agents, the files of photos and brochures and your correspondence with people you could visit in every country? Would you like a TV with a VCR so you could look at videos of different places? A computer so you could go online and talk to people about the best things to see? Where would they go?

Or what if you preferred to make a film? Where would you keep the camera and other equipment, show the dailies, have meetings with your crew? Maybe you'd like to be a fashion designer? Look around and find a place for your drawing board, your dress dummy and sewing machine, your fabric, your pattern table.

You might want to imagine you're a photographer, or an entrepreneur, a consultant, a traveling speaker, a furniture maker, or a budding politician. Perhaps you'd enjoy running a social club, or a philanthropy. Maybe you'd like to be a cartoonist who writes instructional comic books, or a sculptor who works in marble, or the publisher of a newsletter about whales. Maybe you'd like to start an organization that helps save the environment.

To make the fantasy complete, imagine a year's schedule on the wall and think of a few events that would be written on it: "Fly to Florence to photograph the rooftops for *National Geographic,"* or "Take my ballet troupe through Hungary, Estonia, and Finland," or "Check out the marble in West Virginia quarry." Sit down and look around. Take some time and go into a dream of something you love in operation.

●❖ UNDERLINE ALERT: INTERESTING CAREERS

If any of the careers I mentioned intrigues you, underline it and dogear this page or write a note in your notebook so you can come back and find it. You'll be using everything you underlined to create a Wish Deck in Lesson Nine.

Dreaming is wonderful isn't it? These dreams I'm asking you to have are a little reward for clearing out all that clutter. In a little while you're going to find one you want to turn into a reality—and then you're going to have the space to set it up and the time to do it. And that will be a very big reward.

In the next lesson, you're going to begin the search for your gifts and talents—the next step in finding the work you will love.

LESSON FIVE

Uncover Your Gifts

"A champion runner doesn't even know he's in a race.
He runs because he loves it."

ANONYMOUS

You'd think we'd all know what we are gifted at, wouldn't you? But we don't. We know what we're good at, but that's not always the same thing. You see, gifts are no more than genetic potential and they have to be developed. Unfortunately, it's much more likely that they'll be overlooked—or even belittled. So many forces conspire to hide our talent from us that by the time we're grown we often have nothing to mark their presence but some occasional urges—which we don't feel adequate to follow.

What forces am I talking about? One is the simple ignorance of adults when it comes to the talents in children. Very few families understand the gifts of their offspring. For the most part our families don't know what to make of us. The first thing a practical society or family does is to teach you what they think is important and make you forget or undervalue what you think is important. If an accountant's child loves to paint, the accountant might not pay much attention—he doesn't know what to look for. Without some kind of positive reaction, the child doesn't consider painting a big deal

97

either—although he may have a very special eye. Left alone, the child might still paint, but he isn't going to be left alone. He's going to be encouraged to forget that silly stuff and learn how to become an accountant.

Schools don't usually help either. They're in the business of teaching you the skills you need to get by in your culture, not of searching out your hidden gifts. A few very special teachers will try, God bless them, and sometimes they make a crucial difference. More often, however, their insights are lost under all the other pressures placed on a child.

So by and large, no one is in charge of developing talent. And the loss to society is impossible to estimate. That's the bad news.

The good news is that the talent inside you is still intact. Your gifts are hiding out in absolutely perfect condition, ready to be developed anytime you're ready. That time is coming very soon, so now is the right moment to begin the search for your gifts. In Lesson Five you're going to look for the clues your talent has left behind. They're lying right out in the open if you only know how to look for them. All you need to do is remember what you used to love.

Lesson Five:
Uncover Your Gifts

If you've been using all the tricks in Lesson Four to clear your decks for action, you should be seeing a lot more space and time in your life. Pretty soon you're going to have plenty of room to work on a dream. But what is that dream? What's the right thing for you to be doing? Should you be an architect or a travel guide, should you save a rain forest or invent a new compass, should you teach children or be an art historian?

You can't ask anyone else for the answer, because they don't know. I bet you think you don't know either—*but you do*. You should be doing what you're gifted at. Not what you're skilled at. Skills are often nothing more than abilities that were developed because they were useful. Like fast typing, these skills may be very useful, but they don't necessarily indicate gifts.

How do you know what you're gifted at? Simple. Just take a look at everything you have ever enjoyed doing in your life— whether you were skilled at it or not.

Yes, I said everything.

How many times have you become fascinated by something—an animal, a building, a car, a work of art, a fresh breeze— and found that the people around you weren't fascinated at all? That's because you were born with special senses for everything you enjoy. What you'll be happiest doing is built into your nature like flying is built into a bird's. That's why talents are called "gifts." They're presents you've been given by nature. *Living a life you will love means using as many of those gifts as you can find time for, and using the most important ones to the limit.*

So, what do you love? What did you ever love?

You're about to take a surprising journey into the past—and the future.

Exercise 1: Tracking What You Loved

Anything you enjoy points to a talent. You may not be willing to go along with such a sweeping statement yet, but I think you'll change your mind by the end of this lesson. For now, bear with me and start tracking down what you loved. I'm going to ask you to search your past for information about everything you've enjoyed since childhood. You have left clues all your life, but learning to be grown-ups trains most of us to pay not the slightest attention to them. After all, who cares if you loved dogs, sang in front of the mirror, read science fiction, and wanted to play in the water for hours?

You do. More than you may understand.

If you think that every kid likes to do the same things, think again. Lots of kids have completely different preferences. Even when they do like the same things you did, they each have their own unique reasons for it. And you had yours. The two questions I ask my clients more often than any others are: "What do you love to do?" and "Why do you love it?" The answer to the first question is rarely surprising; they love to travel or do research, or garden or work with color. But I'm never prepared for the answer to the second question, because *no two people love something for the same reason.* And the reason they love it is the major clue to their originality, their unique viewpoint. Their gifts.

When I point that out, when I tell them they obviously have a gift for color, or being in new cultures, or enjoying science fiction, or swimming, or understanding dogs—they usually say, "Well, you can't build a career on that."

Of course, they're completely wrong. They could if they wanted to, and so could you. You may never choose to become a dog breeder, a professional singer, a science fiction writer or an Olympic swimmer, but figuring out why you love the idea of those professions is going to lead us straight to what you *will* want to do.

Every time you name something you loved in your past, and say why you loved it, you're draping a piece of cloth over an invisible armature. It's like putting clothes on the Invisible Man; soon you're going to see a shape you never knew existed. That figure is your genius, your original vision, your special sensibilities. In this lesson you'll learn how to find these gifts and use them to discover what you want to do with your life.

So find a comfortable place to sit, open your notebook, and get ready to do some remembering.

Part 1: Write something you loved at the top of each page

Think back to three periods in your life: your childhood, your adolescence, and your young adulthood. I want you to remember anything you enjoyed doing from each period. Start with your childhood. You might include petting your cat, being read to, riding your bike, visiting your granddad, watching a lightning storm—*anything* you enjoyed. You can use the example on page 102 to guide you.

(1) Title each sheet with the activity. For instance, "petting my cat" could go at the top of one, "being read to" on another, "visiting my granddad" on a third. Use as many pieces of paper as you need and think up as many titles as you can. Leave the rest of each sheet blank.

SAMPLE ACTIVITY SHEET (LESSON 5)

(Helena)

(1) Riding My Bike

What I Loved
Most

(2) —Freedom
—Getting Away
—Being Outdoors

Themes

(3) Need to be
independent, see
new places

(4a) My Fabulous
Career

(4b) Seeing the world
Having my
name in print,
my picture in
the press

Worldwide bike
touring
My name in travel
mags
Photographed for
bike ads
Became famous

(4c) Fame is very
important to me

(5) Five Years Later

Mountain Explorer
Travel in Afghanistan
Send tapes to mags
Draw maps for
geological societies

(6) Another Five
Years

Teach geography in
a beautiful small
college and lead
tours to the
mountains once
a year

Now think about your adolescence. What did you enjoy then? Start heading more sheets with such titles as "driving a car," "hanging out with friends," "playing computer games," "playing the guitar." When you've titled as many pages as you can, move into your young adulthood, the time when you first moved out into the world. What did you enjoy most in those years? Travel? Geology? Film editing? Fixing cars? Dancing?

Try to think of at least three things you enjoyed in each of these three periods of your life and give each a page of its own. If you manage to come up with more than three activities for each period, go for it! Finish this exercise and I'll tell you what to do next.

Part 2: What I loved most about each activity

Now, I want you to do some writing in the left margin of each sheet.

(2) Write the heading "What I loved most" at the top of the left margin. Now, take a look at the title on each page and ask yourself: what did I love most about that activity? This part isn't easy. You may never have asked yourself *why* you enjoyed doing something. So take some time to think about the answer.

Let's say your title, like Helena's, was "Riding my bike." In the left margin, you'll write some brief notes. If what you loved most was the freedom of it—just getting away from your house and riding through the fields, you'd write, "Freedom, getting away, being outdoors."

Here's what some other people did:

Althea titled one sheet "Hiding out and listening to grown-ups talk." She realized that what she loved was finding out how they thought, hearing how they acted with each other, noticing how they sometimes defended the underdog and at other times were critical. In the left margin she wrote, "seeing what makes people tick," and "the drama of it."

Jay's first title was "Playing with my cat." What he loved most about it was, "that my cat trusted me and didn't trust everybody. I was proud of myself that I was really good to her."

Melanie wrote "Singing while I did the dishes." What she loved most: "Imagining I was a fantastic singing star and held my audiences spellbound."

Write what you loved about each activity in the left hand margin of every sheet.

Think hard. This is the most important part of this exercise—*it might be the most important part of this entire book*—and I promise you will be richly repaid for your effort.

Part 3: In the right margin: Themes

After you have completed Part 2, you're going to see some themes repeating themselves.

(3) Go back to the first sheet and at the top of the right-hand margin, write this heading: "Themes." Now, write your insights under that heading. Keep these margin comments brief. You might get an important insight to yourself, as Jay did:

"When I looked at what I loved most about petting my cat, that she trusted me and I was good to her, I realized that I wanted desperately to be more important when I was a little kid. Makes sense, I was the baby in the family and no one ever listened to me."

Jay wrote in the right-hand margin, "Needed to be trusted, important."

Melanie: "I believed every word of every song I sang. I wanted to sing my heart out to an audience so I could touch their hearts and show them I understood their problems. But I wanted a big crowd. I wanted to reach lots and lots of people."

Her insight was, "Touch the hearts of lots of people."

Give it some thought and see what your writing taught you about yourself.

You're going to start seeing how everything you ever loved doing had a very personal, very strong purpose behind it.

Althea did. "There's a real thread here I never saw before. In childhood I liked eavesdropping on adults. In adolescence I was a total movie nut, and in college I tried acting. I really liked writing and directing plays. All of it is about dialogue, what's going on inside people as shown by how they talk to each other. That interest was there since the very beginning!"

➽ MEMORY DECK ALERT: TITLE EACH CARD

Before you continue with the rest of the exercise, I want you to stop and pull out some blank 3 × 5 cards from your Memory Deck. On each card copy the title from every sheet. If you had nine sheets, you'll write on nine cards. If you want to add other activities you enjoyed in your past, write them on cards, too. Just remember to add the new title to a new page in your notebook as well and complete all the steps: writing why you loved it, and what you learned about yourself.

When you're finished, put these cards aside. You won't need them again until the last part of this chapter, but I want you to create them while everything's still fresh in your mind.

Part 4: Take it to the limit

Now we're going to change direction. I hope these exercises are giving you some insight into what you love and what seems to be important to you. But you still may think that petting one's cat can't lead to a real career or even a lifestyle. *You couldn't be more mistaken.* Listen, nature created you, and nature wasn't fooling around. Nothing you love is there without a reason.

"But what's the significance of loving to ride my bike as a kid? I can't make a living riding a bike!"

No? Bicycles are big business. People are riding them, designing them, writing about them, manufacturing them and selling them every day.

A few years ago a woman told me the only thing she really loved was gorillas.

"So I love gorillas. I can't make a living working with gorillas!"

But she joined the Gorilla Foundation, volunteered at the zoo, and became a gorilla keeper a year later.

Of course, you may not want to turn your love of your pet into a career, but you need to know it's been done, and that if you chose you could do it, too. The problem is that most of us have limited our imagination to what we have been told is possible—and usually we've been told by people without much experience. When you think about it, hardly an activity exists that couldn't become a career. On the credits of the film *Arachniphobia,* after "editor," and "makeup," is the unexpected designation, "spider wrangler." Yes, that's what I said, spider wrangler. Somebody is getting paid to wrangle spiders, and it's a sure bet that this somebody liked spiders as a child.

I want you to leave the ranks of those people who got practical too early in the game, and shake off the notion that there's no way to make a life from what you love. You don't know that at all, and by the end of this chapter you may see things quite differently.

Let's loosen up your imagination right now with Part 4 of this exercise. Open your notebook. You're going to do some more writing on those sheets.

Now, take it to the limit.

Here's what I want you to do. One at a time, take each page and read what you wrote on it. Let's say on the first sheet you wrote "Ride My Bicycle," as your title, and "Freedom, getting away, being outdoors" as why you loved it, and "need to be independent, see new places," under themes in the right margin.

Now, try to imagine that you have focused entirely on bike riding all your life, that you single-mindedly threw your whole heart and all your time into it, that you have turned it into a profession—one that allowed you to be free and independent and see new places—and you have gone straight to the top of that profession. Where would you have wound up? What would your life be like?

(4a) On each page in the center, below the title, write "My fabulous career." While you fantasize, take notes under that heading.

My fabulous career:

Here's what Helena fantasized. "I imagined that I almost became a bike racer until I realized that I didn't really love racing. I don't like the stress, and I wouldn't get to see enough great scenery. So I changed the fantasy. I imagined instead that I rode my bike across the entire country, month after month, just seeing every nook and cranny of the United States. Some bike companies heard about me and asked me to test their bikes and paid me for it. This is how I supported myself. After a while I started being interviewed on TV in a couple of the towns I visited, and I became well known.

"Here's what my life would be like now: I'd travel all over the world, and send tape recordings of my experiences to travel and biking magazines for pay. I'd get photographed for ads for bike companies, too, and people would ask for my autograph.

"For me, that would be the top of the line. That's where my love of biking would have taken me."

While she fantasized, Helena wrote the following: "My Fabulous Career: worldwide bike touring, my name in travel magazines, photographed for bike ads, became famous."

Now, you do what Helena did. Pick up your pen, open your notebook and begin writing. Describe how far each activity could have gone if you had turned it into a career and been totally successful in your own terms. Take it to the limit.

(4b) When you finish, write in the left-hand margin what you loved most about this fantasy. Then go on to the next sheet. On each one, write your fabulous career fantasy and in the left margin, what you loved most about it.

When you've finished writing on all the pages, you'll see that some of the same themes showed up over and over. *And some new themes showed up that weren't there before.*

(4c) Write those themes in the right-hand margins as they occur to you.

Helena was surprised. "I didn't know how much fame meant to me! It kept showing up over and over in the right-hand margins of over half my sheets!"

When you've finished writing on every page, you may be as surprised as Helena. She knows a lot more now about what she needs to make her happy. And that's crucial information, because if you don't uncover the essential elements of what you love, you can wind up discontented and never know why. But often that information won't surface until you force it to by creating a fantasy like this one.

Now Helena knows she has to have recognition in whatever field she chooses. And she could get it in biking—or anything else she loved to do—if she really wanted to.

Helena pulled together elements from her memory that showed her she knew more about careers in biking than she realized. That's not as surprising as it seems, because when you love something, you pay attention when it's discussed. Your ears perk up and you're drawn to every mention of it. Instinctively, you store it away. Helena—like you—has actually become something of an expert in everything she loved without being aware of it.

Nothing about you is irrelevant

All this began with me asking you to list everything you loved to do. I hope it has shown you that nothing about you is irrelevant. Even the smallest pleasure carries important messages about what you are gifted at, what will satisfy you, what direction you could choose. When it comes to designing a life you'll love, you've got to pay attention to *all* the messages that nature has left.

You see, we're like Hansel and Gretel, those children who got lost in the woods in the Brothers Grimm's fairy tale. We, too, left bread crumbs on the trail, markers to help us find our way home, but only you, as an adult, can decipher those markers. Children can't plan careers, and young adults are often following someone else's rules. Maybe that's how so many of us got lost so far from home in the first place. But now you have the opportunity to look over those markers with the respect they deserve—and finally to find your way home.

Part 5: Five years later

(5) Now I want you to do a little more writing. On each sheet, below what you've already written, write another heading: "Five years later." Now, carry your fabulous career fantasy five years into the future and describe where success has carried you.

Take a look at what Helena imagined: "I'm a mountain explorer. After five years of riding around the United States on my bike, I needed even more freedom and wanted to see more new places so I took to traveling in the mountains of Afghanistan where few outsiders had ever been. I attracted a lot of attention, and I still sent back taped descriptions to magazines. I became known as a mountain explorer. Geological societies asked me to draw maps of where I'd been and I found that I loved drawing maps."

Remember Althea, who loved listening in on adult conversations as a child? Here's what she imagined: "First I became a psychiatrist and absolutely loved it. I realized that I not only loved hearing about people's lives, but I loved helping them solve problems. But after five years I wanted to do something more creative so I started writing detective stories and screenplays and selling every one."

Got the idea? Write a paragraph on each page. I won't explain why just yet because as soon as you finish I want you to swing right into Part 6.

Part 6: Another five years later

Don't hate me for this. I have a very good reason for asking you to do this one last exercise in this chapter. Whatever you just wrote on each page, I want you to add another five years to it. Imagine more time has passed and you're doing fine. You're still at the pinnacle, nothing bad has happened, things are really good.

Think carefully. It's five years later. How do you want to

spend your time now? Do you still want to continue doing what you're doing? Or would you rather transform it into something else? *This isn't an easy fantasy to create, but it could be the most important of all.* Take all the time you need.

(6) Write your description on each sheet, or continue on another page if you need it. When you've written everything you can think of, sit back and look at what you've done.

You've just gotten a glimpse into what you really want.

Most people are amazed at what they came up with. I call this last fantasy "Postsuccess Stories." Most of us never think past the point of attaining our dreams. If anything, it makes us slightly uncomfortable to go past "happily ever after." Maybe we fear we'll be bored once we get there, or that it won't be as wonderful as we hoped. But from everything I've seen, those won't be problems. I don't think you'll be bored when you attain your dream, and it will probably be more wonderful than you think.

But there will be more that you want, and some part of you senses it.

This isn't because you picked the wrong dream. Far from it. It's just that the most important parts often can't show up until *after* you have attained what you want. That's probably because our first dreams are meant to fill our most urgent needs. But once those needs are filled—even if it's only in a fantasy—we are free to create dreams based on who we really are.

I have a friend who always wanted to sail around the world, but he could never get around to it. Instead, he was always starting small business ventures and was tied down with endless amounts of stressful work. His fantasy, of course, was that he sailed around the world in his prize-winning sailboat, free as a bird, happy as a porpoise.

And after five years?

"I guess I wouldn't want to stay out there much longer than that. I guess I'd want to come home then and play with another business venture. How disappointing! Does that mean that I don't really want to sail around the world?"

Of course not. It didn't mean that at all. And that's what he discovered in the second "After five years" fantasy.

"I almost started laughing," he said. "After another five years, what I wanted was to go back to sea! In the interim I had started another business and had a lot of fun—that was a revelation in itself—but then I'd had enough and wanted to go sailing again!" What did he learn about himself? Number one, that he didn't want to live the rest of his life on a sailboat, but that he did want to sail around the world. "I think that's why I never put a serious plan into action. I thought I was going to have to say good-bye to this life forever and some part of me didn't want to do that." Number two, he realized he loved business. "I thought I hated the stress, but I don't, not really. It's just that after a year or two, I need a good rest. And sailing is my favorite kind of rest."

He is now designing and building a sailboat. His target date for his first around-the-world sailing trip is set for right after he concludes his present business venture.

Here's what Althea found after her second five years had passed. She had gone from listening to adults as a child, to being a psychiatrist, to being a writer of detective stories and screenplays: "After five years of being a great novelist, I think I'd like to be a consultant on a movie—helping with dialogue and motivation. I don't want to write anymore because I want more free time, but I love working with actors and directors because I have such a good sense of how a character feels and what he needs to say. That's my heart talking. If I ever didn't know what I wanted, I think I know now."

Not only does Althea know what she wants, it's not at all impossible to get it. Soon. She could start out as a volunteer consultant to an amateur theater group to gain experience, and eventually, if she's gifted—and by our definition she is—find a place for herself in the world of theater or film.

"I had no idea," she said. "I went all the way around the block to find out what I love and how easy it is to get it."

Surprising, isn't it? Our "postsuccess" stories show us that sometimes the most important information hides in that "happily ever after" time.

I hope these last six exercises have surprised you over and over; and convinced you of my original premise: What you love is what you are gifted at. There is no exception. A lot of talent has been wasted because people didn't understand that. Let me tell you the story of a near miss.

Charles Darwin's father had a career plan for him: he was to be a doctor. Dutifully, Charles went to university to study medicine. But he couldn't get interested in it. Instead, he spent his time going out with fishermen to gather oysters, which he then dissected. He didn't like his university courses but he took taxidermy lessons because he loved hunting. And he loved going for walks with a sponge expert who ardently believed in evolution—but had no idea how it actually worked.

To Darwin's father this did not look good—and Charles agreed with him. "[My father] was very properly vehement against my turning an idle sporting man, which then seemed my probable destination." They both agreed he should become a clergyman.

He changed universities and began to study divinity. And then he was offered an unexpected opportunity: to be the naturalist on the HMS *Beagle*. The rest is history.

Now, when we look back, it makes perfect sense that Charles Darwin wanted to dissect oysters and learn taxidermy and discuss evolution. But at the time, to his father and *to Charles Darwin himself,* that was not at all clear. They both thought he was wasting his time.

You could easily have made the same mistake about yourself

at the beginning of this lesson. But now I think you can see it clearly: nothing about you is irrelevant. What you love is what you are gifted at. There is no exception.

Well, Darwin was saved by going to the Galápagos Islands, and you might be saved by what I'm going to ask you to do now. Pull out those 3 × 5 cards you wrote on right after Part 3 in the most recent Memory Deck alert. You're about to be caught off guard.

Exercise 2: The Shock of Reality

Take a look at every activity you wrote down—and do it. Once. That's right, I want you to put this book down, get out of your easy chair and get into action. And don't stop doing what's on those cards—try one each week—even if it takes you a year.

Don't worry, you don't have to quit your job and dedicate yourself to this delightful task full time. But you do have to do at least one activity on those cards each week.

Helena will obviously go for a bike ride this week. "I haven't been on a bike in years!" she said with a laugh. All the better. Then it will take her right back to her childhood. If you wrote "Botany," then you should pull a dandelion from the grass and diagram its inside. If you said, "Go to the movies," try to find a movie of the type you liked when you were younger and go see it.

Is this really so important? You bet it is.

The moment you put imagination into action, everything changes. That's when your physical side joins the party, and your sense memories spring into life. The effect is surprisingly powerful, just as though you had been quietly looking at a musical score and suddenly a symphony orchestra exploded into sound.

Come on, now, you might be saying with disbelief. What if a card says "drawing with a charcoal stick." That's not going to be such a big deal, is it?

You bet it is. Especially if you haven't done it for a long time. The results are stunning. You'll wake up the senses that were fresh and active when you were young, and you'll get a lesson in how shockingly powerful it is to do even the simplest thing you love, instead of just thinking about it.

"Sometimes all I do in a week is spend half of one lunch hour looking at a few pages of a book on theater," said an executive, who loved theater as an adolescent. "It's amazing what an effect such a little thing has had on me. I feel very alive."

"I picked up a pencil and drew a picture of someone sitting across from me on the bus. It was pure heaven! It only took about four minutes! I've been depriving myself of this for years because I thought I didn't have the time!" said a nurse who had been a fine arts major in college.

The actual amount of time you spend doing any activity isn't what matters. All that counts is that you step inside the experience for a moment, just enough to really remember how it feels and to wake up those special sensibilities of yours. The response will be as powerful and delicious as the smell of hot apple pie.

It also doesn't matter how often you do these activities. Just once can be enough. I think most of us believe that if we can't do what we love full-time and permanently, it just isn't worth doing at all. I used to think there was no point in traveling if you couldn't spend an entire year somewhere. But now I know how a wonderful place can get into your soul in just an afternoon.

Even though what you're doing might seem small—going for a swim, going to a dog show, sitting in on a political debate—one of these experiences could hit a nerve that's been asleep for years. Suddenly you'll understand the importance of reawakening a marvelous habit we all had as children: the habit of enjoying yourself with small, potent bits of experience. You knew then, and you need to remember now, that these small joys came from the heart of you, your core, and that's what makes them of primary importance.

The difference between thinking about something and actually doing it is gigantic—no matter how small the activity. You have to practice making that leap from thought to action over and over so that you'll already be accustomed to it when the time comes to go after your big goal.

Until then, your life is going to become exciting out of all proportion to the actual activity you're doing. If you try to tell a friend why drawing for four minutes a day, or rowing a boat on a lake one Saturday, or visiting a lumberyard has turned your life around, they'll never understand. Because they don't love to draw or row a boat like you do. They don't understand what happens to you when you smell fresh-cut lumber.

But you will understand perfectly, because you love it. You'll probably never be able to explain, but it doesn't matter. If ever you follow through on any of these loves, everyone will understand. Just as we now understand Darwin.

Of course, there's always a chance that you can't bring yourself to do anything you wrote on those cards.

I can never do the exercises in these &*#% books!

What happens if you find you can't bring yourself to actually get out there and do those activities you wrote on your 3 × 5 cards? What if you somehow never find time to walk in the woods or write one line of a poem or go horsebackriding even once? If you think that means you've flunked this lesson, I have a confession that might surprise you.

I had a second reason for asking you to swing into action—a secret reason.

I wanted to wake up your resistance.

To see what I mean, turn to Lesson Six.

L E S S O N   S I X

Resistance, or What's Stopping You?

"Because there are two kinds of idleness, they form a great contrast. There is the man who is idle from laziness, and from lack of character, from the baseness of his nature. You may if you like take me for such a one.

"Then there is the other idle man, who is idle in spite of himself, who is inwardly consumed by a great longing for action, who does nothing because he seems to be imprisoned in some cage, because he does not possess what he needs to make him productive, because the fatality of circumstances brings him to that point, such a man does not always know what he could do, but he feels by instinct: yet I am good for something, my life has an aim after all, I know that I might be quite a different man! How can I then be useful, of what service can I be! There is something inside me, what can it be!

"This is quite a different kind of idle man; you may if you like take me for such a one."

VINCENT VAN GOGH, *COMPLETE LETTERS*

"I can never stick to anything. I've tried before and always failed."

"I'm a procrastinator. I don't know why."

"I can work like a horse on things that don't matter. But when

119

I really want something for me I can't get up the same momentum."

What is wrong with these people—and with the rest of us? Why is it we can't find the drive to go after our dreams and sustain that drive until we get them?

The answer? Resistance. Something inside feels uncomfortable every time we try to do something emotionally risky like pursuing a dream. Even when a dream seems so small and immediate—exercising, doing your homework—that it hardly qualifies as a dream resistance digs in its heels. You may not recognize that your slowdown is resistance. You might think you just lost interest or you're lazy, but that's almost never the case. No, every time you let yourself down it's because something inside has decided to stop you.

This lesson is in two parts. The first part explains what resistance is and why it exists in every one of us. The second part will show you a new way to slip out of its grasp so you can go after a life you will love.

Lesson Six:
Resistance, or
What's Stopping You?

Everything in this book is designed to make you unstoppable. Everything you've learned in the first five lessons—how to find the right kind of motivation for you, how to gather your allies, how to understand your feelings, how to clear the decks for action, and how to discover what you are gifted at—has gotten you ready to take on the biggest problem that stops all of us: resistance. The time has come to take a good look at resistance—examine what it is and why it wants to stop you—and to learn a completely new way to break free of its grip.

Part 1: What Is Resistance?

Whenever you choose to make a big change in your life, especially in the form of learning or accomplishing something just for yourself, you almost always run into a snag. You may start out at full speed, but something always slows you down. You decided to start playing piano again, but you haven't gone near the keyboard for weeks. You want to call your friends and start a book club, but you can't get around to making the phone calls. You know that you could figure out that new program you're dying to use on your computer if you took some time to read the manual, but you just can't make yourself do it. An interruption may come up to make you drop your project and then for some reason you don't feel like picking it up again when the time comes. You procrastinate. Inertia sets in.

But why?

Because a big, invisible force is sapping your energy. This force is called resistance. Resistance moves in every single time you start to really change. Even if you take the best direction in the world, even if you love everything you're trying to do, resistance shows up.

Don't think you're the only one with the problem. Resistance is absolutely universal. You couldn't possibly have a friend who has dieted once, done it perfectly, and never had to diet again. You've never met anyone who started an exercise program and never stopped. Absolutely everyone battles resistance at one time or another.

And that universality is the biggest clue resistance has given us to its nature. We've all been taught that we should be able to forge straight ahead to our goals without hesitation or difficulty, and that if we don't follow through it means we have a structural weakness in our makeup. Our "can-do" culture is at war with resistance and we're taught that when we feel like quitting we must battle that impulse to the death, or we are, quite simply, losers. But if resistance is universal, if it's not an aberration, then you can't assume it's a sign of weakness. It must be as natural and biologically based as sleeping or eating, built into our system for a purpose. I don't think we should rush into combat with it until we figure out what that purpose is.

The bodyguard that runs your life

If you think your inability to stick with your resolutions is a sign of weakness, I have a surprise for you: it's more likely a sign of strength. No question about it, resistance is very inconvenient, and it definitely gets in your way. In this chapter you're going to learn how to handle it so it doesn't stop you. *But don't for a moment think that resistance is some kind of weakness.* It's stronger than you and all your culture's "can-do" messages combined.

That's because resistance is a primitive safety mechanism, like a big, muscular bodyguard pulling you back from what it perceives as danger.

Every instinct you have pulls back from the unknown. It's a reaction handed down in your genetic structure by your Stone Age ancestors—and their ancestors before them. If there was one thing Stone Age people didn't like, it was adventures into the unknown. Life was precarious enough without them. Like any animal, what early humans wanted most was safety. They felt content sitting around with nothing to do because that meant having nothing to worry about; there was enough food for a while, and no danger was approaching.

Of course, they were curious people just as we are and some-times some of them gave in to their curiosity, venturing out far from the safety of the hearth into unfamiliar places. These curious ones were more likely to run into trouble and have shorter lives—and therefore produce and raise fewer babies. Those who resisted their curiosity, however, who were content when they were at rest, usually lived longer. They would be more likely to have babies and live long enough to raise them until they could have babies of their own, allowing this resistance trait to continue to be passed down.

The chances are pretty good that our ancestors are the ones with the resistance.

So you see, resistance is almost certainly coded into your

genes. It's your inheritance, handed down to you from your ancestors, and it wants to prevent you from doing new and interesting things simply because it's afraid you'll lose your footing and get into trouble. Resistance has one goal: for you to live in safety.

It can't comprehend why you want to do anything as difficult and unpredictable as audition for an acting job, make sales calls, stand up in front of people and give a speech.

It also wants you fat.

You see, resistance wants you to conserve calories to see you through potential famine. So it makes exertion mildly unpleasant. From its viewpoint, doing anything but getting food and running away from tigers is a foolish waste of energy. That's why breaking out of inertia and jumping into exercise or dieting is so hard. When you try to use up calories with exercise or limit them with diet, your survival mechanism thinks you're crazy and throws itself full force into stopping you. The mandate to survive tries to stop you from endangering the life of a Stone Age person—that is, doing anything difficult and unpredictable. And don't think you can tell a gene that the Stone Age is long gone. It can't hear you and wouldn't believe you if it could.

You can't just ignore resistance either. It's up to serious business. If you become adept at fighting resistance, it will come up with any number of clever disguises to keep you from even detecting its presence.

Let's take a look at some of the many disguises of resistance

Disguise 1: You think you're too busy

Being too busy to do the things you want is usually a cloak for resistance. If you think you're too busy, check out how much time you've wasted lately watching TV shows you don't like or staying on the phone with someone when neither of you had much to say.

Disguise 2: You're probably just lazy

Most of us have been taught to think that when we avoid doing what we should it's because we're lazy. Of course, there is no such thing as laziness. It does not exist. If you were in the mood for a hot fudge sundae on a rainy night, you'd probably find all the energy you needed. A truly lazy person would be lazy all the time, so if you're only feeling lazy selectively, you don't pass the lazy test. It's got to be something else.

Disguise 3: Maybe you don't really want it badly enough

Someone recently said to me, "I think exercise is such a pain. I just don't want to put out the effort. I'm ashamed of myself and I know I'll never get anywhere this way. Maybe I just don't want it enough."

If you really wanted to do something badly enough you'd be doing it, right?

Wrong.

Sometimes, the very fact that you want to achieve your goal so much is what's making you not pursue it. Your most important desires can be so loaded with hidden undercurrents that the whole survival side of you simply refuses to let you go near them. Getting high marks in school, becoming the best athlete, going whole-heartedly after anything you know would make you happy might dredge up buried emotions and inner conflicts that your survival mechanisms want no part of. Resistance knows that even when you don't.

Disguise 4: You suddenly get bored

Nothing is weirder than boredom. Anything we don't understand normally intrigues us, especially anything we enjoy. If you were enthusiastically involved in a project and suddenly became bored, *something turned you off.* That mysterious something is resistance. Every time.

Disguise 5: You have more important things to attend to

We've trained ourselves to think, "Grown-ups do the important stuff first, and when they're finished they do what they love." Now, I can see why you might want to act like that when you're interviewing for a job, or expecting a visit from your boss, but why would you suddenly become such a practical, serious person when you were only going to pick up your trumpet or write a short story? You've done what a child might do if it wanted to feel in control: you've lowered your fear level by acting "like a grown-up." That's merely a way of pushing away your uneasiness about taking a risk. Nope, sorry, suddenly thinking you have more important things to do is just another disguise for resistance.

Exercise 1: What Is Your Resistance Style?

Did you find yourself in the paragraphs above? When you're about to go after something you want, does one of these disguises suddenly appear and pull you off track? Open your notebook and start writing down the disguise your resistance typically takes.

Here's what some people said:

Lila: It was very funny to see that list. It made me laugh like I had just gotten caught doing something wrong. I always say I'm too busy to start sewing up my dress designs, but I still manage to find time for television!

Jake: I can't make myself sit down to write my grant proposal. It feels like so much work I get tired just thinking about it. I thought I was lazy, but I'll clean the whole house to avoid writing that proposal!

Martin: When I have something I'm avoiding I get on the phone, and stay on. I'll call anybody. Then the time is gone and I think, "If I just had more time I'd start right now. Who am I kidding?"

Well, if you know all these disguises are nothing but cloaks for resistance, why not bust through them and get into action?

Because that rarely works—at least, not for long. *If you won't stop, resistance will create stress until you do.* Try an experiment and you'll see what I mean.

Exercise 2: Test the Stress Theory

You don't need to do any writing for this exercise. Simply think of a project you've been avoiding, one you actually want to do but never find the time for, *then stand up and move toward it as if you intend to do it.* Walk slowly over to the piano or the computer or the telephone right now. Don't listen to the voices that tell you to stop. And as you take one step after another *notice what you are feeling.*

Can you feel tension rising up inside you? Your resistance is sensing danger and filling you with stress to make you turn back! You might successfully fight that stress once or twice, but sooner or later it will wear you down. *It's almost impossible to single-handedly force yourself to tolerate that kind of stress for very long.* Your body won't let you.

We all do stressful things every day of our lives, of course, but only because we have a boss or a deadline or a top sergeant who will exert a force *stronger* than our resistance and make us complete a project we'd avoid if left to our own devices. We rarely have the kind of willpower needed to overcome resistance on our own. That's why we're able do so many things for other people, but somehow we can't find the energy to pursue our own goals.

This survival part of you has made stress so unpleasant that your every impulse wants it to go away. We've even developed ingenious ways of reducing our feelings of stress. We call them "bad habits." When you open a pint of ice cream or a quart of beer and kill hours channel surfing in front of the TV set you know that nothing good will come of it—but you do it anyway. Because bad habits are fantastically efficient stress reducers. That's what draws us to them.

Bad habits work like pain pills or tranquilizers. They dull the discomfort and make our minds go into a slight trance. I call this state an "inertia dream." This inertia dream we fall into is why we're willing to waste an evening eating or drinking junk we don't need and watching shows we don't care about. We partially check out of consciousness, our blood pressure drops, our survival mechanisms heave a sigh of relief and resistance takes a nap. We're half aware that we're going to regret what we're doing but we do it anyway because it makes us feel safe.

Now the question is: are we happy?

After the ice cream or beer is gone, after we've logged too many hours in front of that TV set, we come out of the dream—and then *we get sad.* We're not full of stress anymore, that's been taken care of. But we know we've dropped the ball; we know we're going nowhere. We hear that little nagging voice telling us that time is passing and we're not doing anything that really matters to us. Once again, when we weren't looking, the invisible force pushed us back into an inertia dream.

You must have low self-esteem, right?

After all, successful people don't cave in to resistance as you do, so maybe some sick part of you hates yourself and wants you to be a loser. Is that what's going on here?

On the contrary. Resistance is clear evidence of high self-esteem. It shows that on the deepest level, you intend to survive. And trust me, successful people know all about resistance, they've just developed ways to get around it (like hiring trainers and managers and secretaries and having deadlines to keep them moving).

Resistance also indicates a strong impulse toward individuality and self-determination, protecting your ego from new, risky ideas. This resistance to outside influences represents your integrity, the proud side of you that doesn't intend to be controlled. It says, "I already have opinions, I'm already valuable; my mind already knows what it thinks." When a two-year-old starts to say "no," it is revealing a sense of itself as a separate individual with personal preferences and choices.

No question about it. Resistance has found a home in us and it's here to stay.

Take a look at the Memory Deck card you wrote in Lesson One. We discussed all the techniques that don't motivate you to stick with your New Year's resolutions, remember? *You didn't know it then, but what we were talking about was resistance.* In that exercise, you discovered that you couldn't get resistance to go away by talking to yourself, or that you couldn't ignore it, or shame yourself into forcing action—and now you can see why.

So forget about guilt. We think if we're punishing ourselves with guilt it somehow makes us more virtuous. After all, we may be bad but at least we're not proud of it. But virtue and badness are not only irrelevant, they're illusions. Guilt doesn't make you virtuous.

You're not bad either, because you couldn't help yourself.

Let me make this very clear: if you could have stuck to your New Year's resolutions—or anything else you wanted to do—*you would have.* I'm not trying to get you off the hook. As a matter of fact, it's hard to face the fact that you don't have the kind of power you'd like to have—not against resistance.

So does that mean we should just give up?

Absolutely not. There is a way to slip out of the grasp of resistance so you can go after a good life.

Part 2: How to Trick Resistance at Its Own Game

Resistance may have the muscle, but you've got the brains. You're about to learn how to slip past resistance. First you'll outwit it by making it think it has won. And then when resistance relaxes, you're going to call up a challenger from inside you as strong and as much a part of survival as resistance itself.

Two states of consciousness

Let's talk about the "inertia dream" for a moment. You need a clear understanding of this powerful strategy that resistance pulls on you before you can create your counterstrategy.

Have you ever been asleep and had one of those dreams where you're trying very hard to wake up but your eyes just won't open? It's as though gravity is pulling you down into dreamland. Dragging yourself awake seems impossible. When you're in a state of resistance, you're in a similar kind of dream. Inertia is one state of consciousness and enthusiastic action is another—and they are as different as being asleep and being awake. The inertia dream behaves a lot like a drug addiction. When you're an addicted cigarette smoker, you're incapable of truly *desiring* to quit. You only *wish* you desired to quit. Trying to act on that wish is exactly like trying to wake up from a deep dream.

And yet, if you somehow manage to quit smoking you look back on yourself with amazement. It's as though you were trapped in a different universe with no ability to see through the fog to *how much you were going to love not smoking!* Our inertia dreams work exactly the same way. When we're caught in an inertia dream we can't remember how much we would love waking up. If only we could remember the desire that resistance wants us to forget!

Well, we can. There is a way to take that model of physical addiction and use it to break out of our emotional inertia dream. Nature left a loophole that we can use to penetrate any inertia dream with desire strong enough to make us want to wake up.

Exercise 3: How to Wake From the Dream

The first thing you have to do is loosen resistance's grip. If you can make it think you're not doing anything dangerous, resistance will relax and let you come halfway out of the inertia dream.

Resistance Strategy Part 1: Find the smallest unit—and do it.

If you're like me, you've got this notion that if you're going to do something important, you should do a *lot* of it. You should study *every* night, you should make *a hundred* sales calls this week, or you should exercise for *hours* a day. That notion alone is enough to sabotage your efforts right at the start, because trying to do something so ambitious all at once is like shouting in the ear of resistance, "Wake up and stop me, now!" And when resistance wakes up, you've got trouble.

A writing teacher I had in Montana once said to my class, "Try to write every day, and if you can't, try to edit every day. If you can't do that, well then just pick the manuscript up in your hand every day and walk around the room with it for a while." Wise words from an artisan of a craft that knows a lot about blocks. Maybe you can't always do what you should, *but you must do what you can.*

And that's what I call the smallest unit. It's a unit of activity so modest that it doesn't threaten resistance.

Physical exercise is a perfect activity to demonstrate this concept. Now, most fitness teachers know they're up against inertia, so they tell you to start small, to exercise for a short time at first— and work your way up until you're doing enough exercise to affect your body. *But how small do you start?* A fitness teacher might tell you to begin with fifteen minutes and gradually move up to forty-five. That might work, but often it doesn't. Why? Because fifteen minutes of exercise could be just enough to wake up your resistance. *You need to start with a unit of exercise so small that your resistance won't even notice it.* And how do you know what that is?

By your feelings.

If you think, "I should exercise for fifteen minutes right now, (or play the piano, or study, or make sales calls) but I just don't want to," that unit is too big. Try to think of a unit small enough to give you *a feeling of complete willingness.* That might be two minutes. Or thirty seconds. Or the unit might have to be even smaller. Maybe the only action small enough to sneak beneath the radar of your resistance is stretching every muscle in your body for a just few seconds, or playing only two chords on the piano, or opening your textbook to the right page and then putting it right back down on the desk. If your response to such a unit is, "Oh, that's not so bad. I can do that right now," then you've found the right size to start with. That's what I call "the smallest unit."

> **✦ MEMORY DECK ALERT**
>
> **Take out a blank card from your Memory Deck and write the name of your project at the top, "Study for Real Estate Exam," "Interview relatives for family history," or whatever. Then, directly under the heading, write the smallest unit you're quite willing to do at this moment. If you feel you won't study more than thirty seconds then that's the unit you must pick.**

And then you should study for thirty seconds.

And then you should stop.

You'll be tempted to do more, and you might succeed in studying for an hour, but then tomorrow you won't be able to study at all. So restrain yourself at first. Remember, our goal is to avoid alerting resistance at all.

Right now I bet you're saying something like, "Hold it! Thirty seconds of studying won't do me any good!" And neither will thirty seconds of piano practice or thirty seconds of exercise, right? Wrong.

*A half minute of exercise may not do your cardiovascular system, or your grade point average or your piano repertoire any good—but it will do **you** a world of good.*

Because any amount of piano practice will make you remember you love music. And any amount of studying will make you remember you love learning. Even ten seconds of exercise will remind you how good exercise feels. You don't believe me? Hold this book in your left hand so you can keep reading and exercise your right arm for ten seconds. Then switch hands and exercise your left arm for ten seconds. Then stretch and exercise each leg for ten seconds. What are you feeling? The pleasant tingle of your muscles and nerves waking up and your lungs pulling in some extra oxygen. No anxiety or stress.

You don't feel any stress because you've slipped past the watchful gaze of resistance. Resistance isn't worried about thirty seconds of exercise. It thinks you're still safely in your inertia dream. As long as you keep your exercise unit very small, you won't feel any danger. And the same thing goes for any project you're doing.

Say you always want to go swimming but the water is too cold, so you sit by the side of the lake and dangle your feet in the water for a while. It will only take a certain amount of time before you remember how much you love swimming. You'd still be half asleep, but you'd be setting the scene for desire.

When you start getting accustomed to these pleasant feelings you might even get away with increasing the duration of what you're doing. Resistance is more tolerant of activities that are familiar. But don't get cocky or reckless when you're dealing with resistance. If you overstep your comfort limits, you'll pay for it next time around.

The point of this first strategy is not to increase the duration of work you're doing, but to lower the danger level just enough so you can begin to recall how good it feels to do what you love.

And then the balance between resistance and action will begin to tip.

At some point that delicious little bit of water around your feet might make you want to swim *more* than you want to be warm. And then you'd have another part of the strategy to perform. But before I tell you what that is, we have to take care of a problem that could easily surface.

You don't feel like doing even the smallest unit.

You don't want to dip your toe in the water, or open your textbook, or sit down at the piano. No unit is so small that you're comfortable doing it. Resistance has shown up on the smallest level.

What do you do then? There's only one way to avoid defeat. *You refuse.*

Resistance Strategy Part 2: If you can't beat them, join them.

If resistance won't let you do even the smallest unit, don't get in a tug-of-war, and don't slink off to the refrigerator to dull your shame with comfort food. Stand up and declare your refusal to do anything at all today.

That's right. Put your foot down and just say "no."

This is very important. It may seem very peculiar to refuse to do something no one is making you do but that's exactly what I'm suggesting. Don't slink off in defeat, stand up in defiance. You must absolutely take charge and refuse to do a thing! Announce to yourself, out loud if possible, "I refuse to do this today, and that's that." It may sound stupid but it's going to save your dream. Here's why.

You'll be in charge. You'll have made an energetic choice, not have been whipped in a battle. You won't have pushed your project to the back of your mind so it can't shame you—you'll be too defiant to be ashamed. Anyway, you haven't dropped the project. You've simply refused to do it that day. And if you don't want to do it the next day, make your announcement again. Anytime you can't do the smallest unit, it's crucial that you declare your refusal.

But hasn't resistance actually won again? Not exactly, because you have co-opted the defense mechanism, gotten the jump on it, thrown the game out of balance. Resistance hasn't lost, that's true. But neither have you, and that's going to turn the whole thing around.

You see, even if you refuse to exercise or to play piano or to write your novel *every day for weeks or even months,* you'll be doing more to attain your goal than if you helplessly let it slip into oblivion. It may seem odd to be in charge of nothing more than refusing, but it's essential that you're in charge. It will prevent the inertia dream from creeping up around you like a fog and lulling you into passivity. Instead, you will stay wide awake and completely active.

What will your survival mechanism make of this new behavior? Sooner or later resistance will decide you're a very strange creature, but since you seem to be out of danger it will go back to sleep. After enough days of clearly announcing that you absolutely refuse to write even one line of your novel, one morning you'll probably sit down and start writing without much fuss at all.

Until that time, however, if you find you can't do even the smallest unit, fold your arms, stick out your jaw and refuse. When you're ready to get started again, move on to the third part of this resistance strategy.

Resistance Strategy Part 3: Declare your love for the smallest unit.

Now that you've identified a unit small enough that you're completely willing to do it, there's something you should know: you love it. It may not be immediately obvious, but it's true. That's a guarantee.

You can't force love—and you don't have to.

Never try to make yourself love the smallest unit. Never look at that manuscript you're carrying around and say, "Okay, I love you, I love you," as if saying it over and over would make it true. That's fake and it won't work. As a matter of fact, trying to make yourself love something will drive any real love you feel into hiding. *You don't have to force yourself to love the smallest unit, because you already do. If you love the dream, you always love the details of it. It's impossible that you won't.* Let me illustrate with a story.

One day, a violinist friend of mine was practicing at my house because her house was being painted. I was going about my business when all at once she started to play, very slowly, the most gorgeous tune I have ever heard in my life. It was so beautiful, I just stopped and listened. There was a moment of silence when she finished and then she played the same simple, ravishing melody again. I walked closer and tiptoed into the room to watch her play. Her eyes were closed. She was completely absorbed with the sounds coming out of her violin. Again, she played the same amazing melody, note by note, slowly and lovingly.

When she was finished she opened her eyes and looked calmly at me.

"Joanna," I said, "what on earth was that incredible melody?"

"I was just playing the scales," she said, smiling.

I was stunned. "The scales! You mean do re me? That's all you were playing? I can't believe it. It was so beautiful!"

"I know. It's the best tune ever written," she said.

I thought scales were like sit-ups. I thought musicians practiced the scales because they had to, to strengthen their muscles. But Joanna changed my mind forever.

"Scales are a miracle. Think about it—all music is in them," she said.

That's a real musician.

You can find people like Joanna in every field. I saw a documentary not long ago about Chuck Jones, a famous animator—the inventor of Wile E. Coyote and Roadrunner. Someone on camera said—I have to paraphrase—"Chuck Jones loves every single frame he draws as if it were the only one in the world. As if it were a Rembrandt."

When Chuck Jones came on camera he was a little embarrassed by this observation but he confessed that it was true, and his embarrassment disappeared as he spoke. "You have to love the smallest part of what you do or you'll never be any good at anything. If you don't love it, you're in the wrong field. A real musician loves every dotted eighth note and I love every animation frame."

And if you take a look at the smallest unit of anything you're gifted at, you too will feel that kind of love. That's how you know you have a gift. The smallest part is so beautiful to you it draws you like a magnet. As a famous architect once said, "God is in the details."

━ MEMORY DECK ALERT

On the 3 × 5 card you've been writing on, add why you love doing this small unit. If you think of more than one reason, be sure to write them down, too. You can't love too many things about the smallest unit.

Love the smallest unit and desire will pull you right out of your inertia dream.

If you're willing to sit by the side of the lake and splash your toes around in the cold water, you're going to remember how much you love water on your feet. That's when desire will come on the scene. Desire not only has the strength to challenge resistance, it *wants* to. They're natural enemies. Where resistance wants you to sit still and play it safe, desire wants you to jump into action. Consider hunger and the powerful desire for food. Danger might make an animal wait a long time to go after food, but eventually hunger will be stronger. Consider romantic love; its ancestor sex and its grandchild adventure. Though none of these is a survival requirement for an individual, they are all very important for the species. For that reason, natural selection has made the desire for sex, love, and adventure so magnetic that unless we are in serious danger, it will draw us out of the safety zone and into action. Because desire is a survival mechanism, too, as natural as resistance.

This is the secret of pulling yourself out of the inertia dream: first lower the danger and then introduce desire.

In the inertia dream, resistance made you forget how much you want to use your gifts. When you do the smallest unit, however, you begin to wake up that desire, without alerting resistance. It's so important to bring this concept home to you, I hope you'll permit me one more example.

Let's pretend your dream is to eat hot apple pie, but you're standing on one side of a cold stream and the hot apple pie is on the other side. You may know in your mind that you want that apple pie but if you can't smell it, all your attention is on how cold that water is. You can't get motivated. You get the blahs and slouch away, ashamed that you don't have the drive to go through the cold water to get what you want.

But if you can get a really good whiff of that apple pie, everything will become unsettled, stirred up. You'll remember how tasty that pie is! Comfort will stop being comfortable and start to feel stifling. Longing will begin to stir and create agitation—and resistance will know it has met its match, desire—a foe more formidable than willpower or self-discipline.

*   *   *

There you are. That's the system in a nutshell. If you follow the strategy part by part, you'll be very impressed with the results. Now we have resistance surrounded.

Or do we?

Resistance's best trick of all: make us forget and then give up.

There's no longer anything resistance can pull on you that you can't handle—except, of course, its best trick of all, a favorite one-two punch called "first forget and then when you remember, feel demoralized and give up." Here's how it goes: You're proceeding comfortably on your project using the strategy you just learned and taking some step toward your goal every day. If it gets difficult, you fall back and do only the smallest unit; and if you can't find a unit small enough, you loudly announce your refusal until you're ready to begin again.

But then something makes you forget to do any of that.

Life intrudes, you get the flu, your in-laws visit for a week—somehow you just forget what you were doing. When you finally remember, you realize a week has passed and your heart sinks into defeat. A voice inside you says, "What's the point in starting up, you'll only forget again."

The forgetting and the voice of defeat are both sent to you by resistance. They're trying to pull you back into the inertia dream. But guess what? I have a way for you to keep from forgetting to do your resistance strategies.

Resistance Strategy 4a:
Create triggers that don't depend on you.

How do you remind yourself to pursue your goal when resistance wants you to forget? With your Memory Deck. Your Memory Deck was designed for just this kind of situation. The only thing you have to do is carry it with you as you carry your keys or your eyeglasses, and to thumb randomly through the cards a few times a day.

Carry a few paper clips with your Memory Deck. You can attach them to a blank card and keep them in the deck. One of them goes on the card you've been writing the whole resistance strategy on. Put a paper clip, even two, on the side of the card so it stands out in the deck. Even if you happen to forget why they're there, the paper clips will signal an important card and remind you to read it.

One woman who was starting her own catering business told me she went through a period when she constantly forgot to make evening sales calls on the phone after getting home from her day job.

"I'd look through my cards during the day, but at night I'd totally forget. It was the strangest thing. Then I'd be just about to go to sleep and realize I'd forgotten again!" she said. "So I started calling my home answering machine during the day and leaving myself a message every time I came across my Memory Card. Then as soon as I got home and listened to my messages, there it was! I'd sit down fast, make my calls and be done with it, before I'd forget again. It actually worked!"

Resistance Strategy 4b:
When you remember, start again.

If you should forget, and you almost certainly will, get back on the program as soon as your Memory Deck or an outside trigger reminds you—and do it without a moment's thought, as if you'd never stopped. Over the long haul, that's the only kind of persistence that makes a real difference; starting up again over and over, every time you notice that you've stopped. Hopefully, resistance will see that its favorite trick of making you forget isn't working and will eventually give up.

But even if it doesn't go away, as long as you always start again as soon as you remember, you'll still be making great progress toward any goal you've set for yourself. *You'll still be unstoppable.*

But what if you forget what you were doing, and you never remember?

Oh, you'll remember. If you love what you are doing it will be as impossible to make you forget forever as it would be for Joanna to forget music forever. You'll remember what you love as you remember the taste of hot apple pie. No problem at all.

Here's a quick review:

When resistance has stopped you from going after a dream:

1) Find the smallest unit you're willing to do, and do it.
2) If you can't do 1), take a stand and refuse to do anything

every day—until you're able to find a unit you're willing to do.

3) Find something you love in this unit, and love it with all your heart.

4a) Protect yourself from forgetting by setting up external triggers to remind yourself.

4b) If you forget to do all of the above, start up again the moment you remember.

Just follow these steps and they will pull you out of inertia every time and into the high energy excitement of going after what you love. *Inside you is all the equipment you will ever need to sidestep resistance.* It's built into your nervous system and stands ready to help you out, but you need to be very alert to pull it into action. These strategies you've just learned are powerful and smart; they'll help you stay alert. After you use them a few times, it will become second nature to go after your goals with a watchful eye on resistance—and a heart full of love.

LESSON SEVEN

The Idea Bank, or Research for the Rest of Us

"Get the facts or the facts will get you."

THOMAS FULLER

✦

"Light is the task where many share the toil."

HOMER

One of the inevitable side effects of going after a goal is that sooner or later you get stymied by a lack of information. Every plan has gaps in it, steps you can't take because you simply don't know how. What you need is a way to research anything you need and that's what Lesson Seven is going to teach you.

Now if you're like me, it takes only the mention of research to send an ice-cold chill up your spine. Visions of dark libraries, ponderous books full of incomprehensible, unreadably small print, and endless searches that send you so far afield you can't remember what you were looking for in the first place is what research

145

always meant to me. I can't teach you that kind of research, and I wouldn't if I could.

But thanks to my own shortcomings and profound lack of discipline, I have developed a series of research techniques that are simple, effective, even jolly. A few of them involve looking in books and magazines, but many will ask only that you talk to other people. One even requires throwing a party! I call my methods "Research for the rest of us." I've included in no particular order every trick I've ever found useful, and you can try them in any combination you like. But do try them. Each one opens a chest full of unexpected treasures just waiting for you.

Lesson Seven:
The Idea Bank, or Research for the Rest of Us

Here are twelve of the most enjoyable ways of getting help and information that I know of. Some are unorthodox, but I've tried them all and every one is first rate!

Idea 1: The wish/obstacle solution

This is probably the simplest and most effective way of getting great ideas that I know of. All it requires is that you tell as many people as possible—friends, colleagues, people on the bus—what your wish is and what obstacle you face. That's all. You simply phrase your problem in that form: first the wish, then the obstacle. Like magic, it triggers an instant need in almost anyone to solve your problem. Here's how it works.

If you only tell someone your wish—say, that you could go to the Himalayas—you may get any sort of response from, "Sounds great!" to "What do you wanna go there for?" On the other hand, if you accompany your wish with a specific obstacle and say, "I'd really love to go to the Himalayas, *but I don't want to go unless I can talk to someone who's been there,*" then whoever you're speaking with is immediately going to spring into problem-solving mode.

It never fails. They'll start rubbing their chin and scratching their head. They'll flip through their address book and maybe even dig out an old college yearbook for you. They'll rack their brains for anybody they've ever known who has been to the Himalayas and, before you know it, your Rolodex will be filled with names of people to call, half of whom are available to speak with you immediately.

Why does the wish/obstacle solution work so well? Because human beings are problem-solving animals. We can't help it. It's in our DNA. When there's a problem, we want to fix it. When there's an obstacle, we want to overcome it. The wish/obstacle puts your dreams and other people's basic human instincts in sync.

Some of the greatest examples are right out of my workshop.

I remember a young woman named Cynthia who stood up one night and said, "I build harps using a certain type of wood from Scotland, but the wood is all gone and I can't get any more of it." Now I don't know a thing about harps, much less about the kind of wood that goes into making them. So I did what I always do at such times: I said, "Does anybody have any ideas for Cynthia?"

Someone immediately jumped up and said, "Yes, there's more of that wood. It's in New Zealand. My brother owns the forest where it comes from. I'll hook you up with him!"

In Greenville, South Carolina, there was Martha who stood up very sheepishly one evening and said, "Well, if you must know, my dream is to dance with Patrick Swayze. But of course I don't know him." Now I don't know Patrick Swayze either, but I asked the group for help, and a woman sitting two seats away from Martha said, "No problem! His mother owns a resort nearby where I work. He comes there all the time. I've danced with him before and if you come up next Thursday, I'll introduce you!"

Martha danced with Patrick Swayze the following Thursday.

Sometimes your problem will be solved immediately and sometimes it won't. But when you start talking to people on a wish/

obstacle level, your whole world will suddenly grow very creative. The more people you talk to, the better chance you have of finding a terrific solution. People will tell you stories about what they've done, what their friends have done, and things you might want to try yourself. You never know what's going to happen, but it's always delightful and, if you pay attention, extremely informative.

The wish/obstacle solution works so well you can even use it with negative people. Although I normally advise against revealing your dreams to anyone who may mock or belittle them, in the case of the wish/obstacle I make an exception. Why? Because the wish/obstacle doesn't rely on goodwill. It's fueled by the inability of our species to let certain ideas stay in suspension. Negative folks included.

Test it out. Present a wish/obstacle to the greatest naysayer you know. What will happen? Nine times out of ten they'll say something like, "What are you, stupid?" or "That's the dumbest idea I ever heard." And then, in their quest to prove their superiority, they'll start producing solutions for you. In fact, the more intense their negativity, the more completely unacceptable it will be for them to fail in solving your problem!

So figure out your own wish/obstacle and pick up the phone. Call a friend—or a critic. Tell it to the checkout clerk in the supermarket. An encyclopedia of information is inside every person we pass on the street and all you have to do to tap into it is strike up a conversation. You'll be amazed at the results.

Idea 2: The Idea Party

This is also a personal favorite of mine. But don't worry. The Idea Party doesn't require you to be a professional caterer or a high-society hostess. In fact, you don't do much preparing for an

Idea Party—you just invite some friends and ask them to bring some of theirs. Everybody seems to find the notion of an Idea Party interesting, even though they're not quite sure what it is.

And tell everybody to bring something to eat.

The Idea Party is a potluck dinner where you invite people into your home for the express purpose of sitting down with a plate of good food and brainstorming on your particular problem.

Why do they bring the food? Because you want them looking around in your kitchen for pots and pans, talking to each other, and helping each other solve problems like "Did you see a casserole dish anywhere?" You also want everything to be very informal, and for everyone to feel like the host, so keep a low profile and don't help them too much when they're preparing the food.

How to get started

Set a time and place and write up your guest list. You want to include anyone who will be supportive, and exclude anyone who might be disruptive or cynical. You also want your friends to bring a few people you don't know at all, some people outside your immediate circle. It's not only a great way to meet new friends, it will expand the range of information in the room by including people from different circles than yours.

Getting down to work

Okay. The evening is now well under way. All the guests have arrived, the food is on the table, and everyone is filling their plates. Now it's time for the group to move into the living room and take seats on the floor because the "idea" part of the party is about to begin.

And it starts with you.

Tell the group your story. Get them involved. Explain how much you've already accomplished and how close you are to the next step. Tell them what you want to do. What approaches you've tried, which worked, which didn't. Tell your whole story, complete with personal struggle and conflict so everyone becomes really involved. Then, when you've got them hooked, present your wish/ obstacle:

"The only thing is, I don't know anyone who's ever been to the Himalayas!"

Now all you have to do is crouch down and play catcher while everyone starts throwing ideas at you! It's terrific fun. Dozens of ideas and solutions will immediately start flying your way. Somebody will have a name for you to contact. Another person will pick up the phone then and there and call someone else. The person you need to meet may even be in the room! The group will tirelessly debate a dozen new approaches you never thought of, each more exciting and original than the next!

But, don't even try writing these ideas down yourself. It's too likely your resistance will creep back in with censoring thoughts like, "Oh, I couldn't do that," or "I couldn't call there." Instead, ask someone to take notes for you. They'll think it's wonderful that you're going to take on all these tough tasks and their support will give you the strength you need to do them!

All of this idea pitching usually takes about an hour, but that does not mean the party is over. Once your problem is solved, move on to someone else. In fact, people will often just stand up on their own and say, "I've been trying to do something for a long time and I wonder if I could run it past the group."

Great! Tell everyone to get dessert and buckle down for the next round. This is what Idea Parties are all about!

So go ahead. Invite ten or fifteen people to your home, enjoy a good potluck dinner, then sit down and see how a friendly, well-fed group of people can move you light years closer to your goal than sitting alone at home ever could.

Idea 3: The library

Now this idea may sound like a contradiction to what I said before, but despite my own difficulties with traditional research, I've found one resource in the library incredibly valuable and I've learned to master it without much difficulty.

It is the Reader's Guide to Periodical Literature.

This reference is a set of books full of the names of all the magazine articles written in every major magazine in the country. If you enjoy reading magazines, this is the most entertaining library research you'll ever do. Just pick a subject you're interested in—say the Himalayas or poetry conferences. Look it up in the guide and you'll see what articles have been written about it in the last few years along with the names of the magazines where you'll find them. Just write down the information you want and give it to your librarian, who will return a few minutes later with your magazines.

Now inevitably some of your articles will not be available. They've either been lost, destroyed, or the library never owned them in the first place. Don't be discouraged. A few articles are sure to be available and that may be all you need. With a pencil and paper, you're now ready to sit down and start taking notes.

As you move through article after article on the same subject, you'll begin to notice that certain kinds of information keep getting repeated. Names. Locations. Ideas. What you're learning is the general shape of your subject. These articles are written for special-interest groups so they'll be quite informative as well as wonderfully readable. All but the most scholarly magazines want their articles to be very accessible to the ordinary reader.

If you're not sure what you want to do, however, or which path you'd like to follow, ask the librarian where the "trade magazines" are stacked. Their titles alone will give you ideas you never would have thought of on your own. You'll find magazines for quilters, cartoonists, dog lovers, boat builders, money managers, nurses, mothers in business, hypnotists, romance writers, astrologists, ventriloquists, and many many more. Each one has articles written especially for insiders and is packed with information. You will also find ads for all kinds of related services, including the dates and locations of the next national conferences.

What if you still want more information? Great. Just call the magazine and ask to speak with the author of the article, or send a letter to the magazine to be forwarded to her. Ask any questions you have. Magazine writers became experts in the subject in order to write about it and invariably have about twenty times more information than appears in their articles. They can give you great leads.

So if there's a field you think you might be interested in, go to your local library, ask for the Guide to Periodical Literature, and get yourself a stack of magazines. It could change your life.

Idea 4: Conferences, associations, trade shows, and expos

When you find conferences listed in the backs of magazines you like, go to them. Don't worry that you'll feel like an outsider. Conferences are full of people who will pull you right in. Conferences for people involved in any craft—especially those that offer classes or lectures—are almost always friendly, informal places. And they make you feel like a craftsperson yourself, no matter how much of a beginner you might be.

Conferences are held for almost every association that exists—and there are literally hundreds of associations. You can find them in an entertaining set of books called the *Encyclopedia of Associations,* one of the most terrific resources around. It is the most complete listing I know of every group and association that meets regularly in the United States. From art clubs to zoology groups, the encyclopedia tells you what they do, where they meet, and how to contact them.

If you're trying to come up with something interesting to do on your vacation, you should know that many associations make it a point to meet in some interesting and beautiful location. It's a great excuse to go somewhere you've never been before and a conference is an insurance policy against being bored while you're there. You're sure to meet lots of friendly people and hear talks about interesting subjects—and usually a cut-rate tour is available so you can see the surrounding countryside.

So check out the conferences. Try them out. They're like an open invitation to hundreds of Idea Parties all around the country.

Trade shows and expos aren't as personal, but they're gold mines of information, the Mardi Gras of resources. If one is taking place that is even remotely related to something I'm interested in, I always go. Why? Because if ever there was a place to find experts who are knowledgeable and willing to talk to you, a trade show is it. These events provide you with direct access to the kinds of people you couldn't meet any other way. And they'll be right in front of you, waiting in the booths, wandering around the aisles. Walk up to any one and start talking. Besides making a friend, you'll get the kind of late-breaking, inside-information you can't find anywhere else.

If you don't know where to look for a trade show in your field, visit your local library and ask the librarian for the Index of Trade Shows. It's easy to use and quite fascinating.

Idea 5: Going on-line

Let's make a leap from the printed page to the new world of electronic media—going on-line with the Information Super Highway. I'll admit this may sound a little high-tech and it isn't right for everybody. But trust me, if I can do it, anybody can.

Basically, going "on-line" means connecting your computer to any one of the many electronic bulletin boards now available or to the Internet—the global network of people and computers hooked up to each other by telephone networks. One of the foremost big bulletin boards is Compuserve, but there are others like America Online and Prodigy, and new ones appear every day.

If it makes you nervous to try to navigate the global superhighway, try something small. Go to a computer store and ask if there's a local bulletin board in your town. These wonderful little pubs-on-computer call themselves "BBS's" (stands for "Bulletin Boards") and many large cities have them. Every evening dozens of local people come on and talk about all kinds of subjects. I find local bulletin boards to be a bit more neighborly and responsible since the members are less anonymous and get together now and then for an "F2F" (also known as a "face to face") at a real pub.

Local BBS's only cost a few dollars a month and you'll find that they are filled with all types of people eager to communicate and exchange all kinds of information. Entirely through your computer. I've seen some wonderful exchanges take place. I remember a request someone put out for a dentist. "I need a good dentist, fast," it read. "I can't pay a lot, but it's got to be a really good dentist." Within twenty-four hours, eleven recommendations were on the bulletin board, complete with descriptions, prices, and telephone numbers.

"How do you move furniture in New York?" read another message. That's it. Just those eight words. Yet within hours that message brought over thirty replies from people telling exactly how they had moved in New York and what moving companies they recommended.

Don't ask me how to connect your computer to the Internet or a local bulletin board, because I have no idea. A friend did it for me and now all I have to do is hit two little buttons. If you don't have a friend like that, I suggest buying a computer magazine to locate one of the many "computer user groups" around. A user group is based on the kind of computer you own—for example a MUG is a Mac User's Group. Join this group if you have a Mac. User's groups are around for IBM PC's and any other computer that's ever been made. These groups need members and you'll never find a more helpful bunch of people in your life. Just walk up to someone with a nice face and say, "I'm sorry, I'm a real dodo, but could you tell me how to go on-line?" You're almost sure to find some very generous people to help you—just find some appropriate way to return the favor.

Going on-line can be a little overwhelming at first, and it isn't right for everyone. The same percentage of angels and cranks show up as do in any neighborhood. But once you get used to it, you'll find you've tapped into the largest, most sensational Idea Party in the world.

Idea 6: The Yellow Pages

This idea is so simple I'm almost embarrassed to mention it, but the Yellow Pages are an amazing resource. Just look up your subject, call anyone even remotely connected with it, and tell them what you're looking for. Don't worry if they aren't knowledgeable or they try to rush you off the phone. Just follow one rule.

Try to never hang up without a lead.

If someone says they can't help you, ask "Where should I go to find out?" If they say they don't know, ask "Do you know anybody who does?" Most of the time you'll get a very helpful person. If someone sounds busy, be thoughtful and say, "Tell me a better time to call you back. I hate to bother you but this is a dead end for me, and I just don't know where to go from here."

Then get real quiet and nine times out of ten they'll realize that it's a real person on your end of the line and try to help you.

The Yellow Pages are not only good for research into something you want, they're good when you don't *know* what you want. What do I mean? Just open the Yellow Pages and start flipping through it. Before you know it, you'll have a dozen ideas for creative projects you could be doing right now and a dozen reminders of ideas you had all along but forgot about. And the phone numbers of the people to contact will be right in front of you!

Idea 7: Salespeople

What kind of people know a lot about a particular subject and are always willing to talk to you about it? Why, salespeople, of course. Suppose, for example, like Cynthia, you wanted to build a harp and you didn't know where to get the wood. What should you do? Go to a lumber yard and talk to the salespeople. Not because they will know about obscure Scottish wood. But because chances are at least one of the salespeople will be intrigued enough to want to talk to you about it and help you look for a solution.

Salespeople often find a great deal of satisfaction assisting with unusual projects. Not only because a sale might result, but because, like most people, they do the same thing day after day and long for change and excitement. Your particular problem offers them the opportunity to perform a special service, one they can take pride in.

So give it a shot, and don't be surprised if you get a phone call a few days later with the name of someone who knows about Scottish wood. Just like making calls from the Yellow Pages, don't end your conversation without a lead. If the salesperson doesn't have the information you need, ask him or her where you might look, and just wait for an answer. You might be directed to someone much closer to the information—and even if the next person isn't right either, he may be closer still. Follow this trail until you have what you need.

Idea 8: Schools

Call every college or adult education program in your area and get a catalog or brochure. You'll find dozens of exciting and terrific courses available. And they're taught by experts, insiders in a field you may want to know more about.

Or try an independent school like the Learning Exchange in Sacramento, an organization that pioneered a program of one-night courses led by a variety of experts. The idea spread like wildfire and now you can find such schools in Minneapolis, Dallas, New York, San Francisco, Seattle, and many other cities. Each school offers literally hundreds of courses, from "How to Make your own Sundial" to "How to Dance HipHop." I often run workshops around the country for these schools, and I think you'll like the students you meet there. They can be a storehouse of information on the subject being taught.

In addition, you will often find the teachers at these programs to be particularly accessible and willing to spend a few minutes talking to you. Just be ready with a clear question that you need answered.

Idea 9: Bookstore treasures

Look in the reference section. You'll not only find dictionaries and foreign language courses here, you'll find a whole college course for writers, from how to write a sonnet to how to write a proposal and find an agent. If you are in a creative field and are looking to sell your stories, paintings, poems, cartoons, or graphic art, there are books designed specifically for you. They're called market books and I consider them essential reading. The one I'm best acquainted with is the *Writer's Market,* which I've found helpful from both an artistic and business standpoint. It lists every publishing house and what they publish, and it includes articles on actual writing techniques. In addition, any new writer will appreciate the book's up-to-date list of literary agents.

The market books tell who's buying artwork or songs or poetry, where you can reach them and what they're paying. They're exciting, informative, and very specific. So go to your local bookstore and walk into the reference section. Look to see if one of these books exists for the subject you're interested in. It's almost as good as having a relative in the business.

Look in the small business section. I have books about how to walk dogs for a living, start a bed & breakfast, be a caterer, a taxi driver, and a handwriting analyst. I got them all in the small business sections of bookstores all over the country. Also try the marketing section. Read at least one chapter in the store before you buy the book. If you don't, chances are it will end up on a shelf, unread, and calling out to you—"read me!"—at least until the next time you remember to Clear the Decks.

Look in any section. Many sections of a bookstore have how-to books in them, so make it a practice to while away an hour now and then, looking at the titles of books in sections you wouldn't ordinarily visit. You might chance upon a gem.

Look in the backs of books. Wander over to any section that interests you—small business, history, religion, women's studies, biographies, or psychology—pick up any book that looks appealing and turn directly to the very back of the book to check out the index. It will be full of topics covered in the book and names of people who've been quoted: although it's only a list, an index can give you an amazing amount of information. In addition, you'll find the bibliography with other books the author recommends on the subject. Before you've read even one word from the main text, you'll start to get a sense of the field you're interested in.

If you want a quick overview of a subject or person, look for the name in the index, open to that page and read the entry. Then move to another book on the same topic. Look in its index for the same name, and read about it in that book, too. After a few searches you'll know facts that were so important no writer left them out, and you'll also get to compare a variety of viewpoints. Although it's just a hint of a beginning, you'll start to understand what it means to be an authority on someone or something, merely by tracking a topic through the indexes.

Idea 10: Write letters

One of the best ways to get information is to write a letter directly to someone renowned in the field. Unfortunately, most people with any degree of prominence also have very little time to respond to such letters. The trick then is to write the kind of letter that catches their eye. I have some unusual insight into this area because I receive lots of letters every week. Now there is no way I could respond to all of them or I would never have time to write any books. However, if someone writes me a well-conceived, interesting, and entertaining letter and seems likeable or interesting, it makes me want to respond. Sometimes I'll just jot a quick note at the bottom of the page and return the letter.

One hint: a specific question you need answered and a stamped self-addressed postcard allows the recipient to answer your letter the moment they read it, before it goes in a huge pile of paper in their "In Box."

Also, whenever you write a letter to somebody famous let them know what you like about her work and that a quick reply at the bottom of your letter would be appreciated. You'll be amazed at what can happen. I know a young filmmaker who wrote such a charming letter to the president of the Walt Disney Company that he was granted the interview he asked for!

Idea 11: Personal ads

You've seen them. "Good-looking so-and-so wants to meet gorgeous such-and-such." Well, why stop at romance when a personal ad offers so many other great opportunities?

Take Emily. She desperately wanted to travel, but she didn't want to go alone. After several months of trying to find a friend to travel with her, she finally decided to place an ad in the personals column. It went like this:

LOOKING TO MEET FRIENDS, HAVE COFFEE AND TALK ABOUT TRAVEL EXPERIENCES ALL OVER THE WORLD. CALL THIS NUMBER . . .

Of course, you must always take precautions when it comes to the personals. Some towns offer temporary answering services to take your calls (look in the Yellow Pages) so you don't have to give out your home or work number. Emily did receive a few calls she'd rather forget, however by using one of these services none of those people can ever reach her again, and most of the responses were from people genuinely interested in travel and intrigued by her ad. Emily now has a group that meets regularly at a local restaurant; they share travel tips and stories, and a few of them have even taken trips together.

I see ads like Emily's all the time. They're for reading groups or film groups or biking groups or art groups. I've even seen ads by people who've read my first book *Wishcraft* and want to form a Success Team. They go like this:

> WISHCRAFT SUCCESS TEAM FORMING. IF YOU'RE INTERESTED, CALL THIS NUMBER . . .

People who respond to this kind of ad have generally read the book and know about Success Teams so you don't have to explain what they are. I know of dozens of Success Teams around the country that were started exactly this way. (However, some people think you're starting a *witchcraft* group, so, if you do this, be prepared for some misunderstandings.)

Try the personals. It's a great way to make new friends and put together a support team for your own dreams and wishes!

● MEMORY DECK ALERT

On a card from your Memory Deck, write a list of *all* these ideas, plus any of your own. You might need a reminder the next time you're stuck.

Conclusion

In the next chapter, I've provided you with a small reference section of your own. It's a sample of personal stories and unusual books and associations, and it includes a hypnotic page full of exotic places to get you started right now on seeing the astonishing range of choices available to you.

That's what I call research. Not so bad, is it? You can probably think of more good ideas yourself. You might even throw an Idea Party to generate them. If you do, let me know what you come up with. I'll pass it around!

LESSON EIGHT

Practice, Practice, or How to Throw Yourself a Dress Rehearsal

> Young woman: "Pardon me, sir. Can you tell me how to get to Carnegie Hall?"
> Old man: "Practice, practice, practice."

Are you ready for some excitement? If you've managed to do the first seven lessons, I guarantee huge rewards from what's coming now. (If you haven't, do this chapter anyway. You'll be glad you did.)

What you're about to do is practice every step of making a wish come true: first, you're going to learn a new way of coming up with delightful wishes. Then you'll try out an unusual method for troubleshooting the obstacles. Finally, you're going to step out into the real world and go after an "impossible dream."

You might accomplish big things in this practice run. It happens all the time. But one thing is for sure: you can't fail. Because attaining the goal isn't the purpose here, gaining experience is. No matter what the outcome, you'll end up a veteran scout, an experienced troubleshooter, a seasoned seeker after great dreams. You can tell who's seasoned and who's not by how they handle unexpected problems: inexperienced people are thrown off balance and need recovery time—they might even drop the project. But seasoned veterans—although they may groan just as loudly at mishaps, calm down faster and move into a problem-solving mode immediately. You need to stumble a little on unexpected bumps in the path and come to expect their inevitable appearance if you're going to become seasoned and unstoppable.

After you've completed this chapter, your chances of making future dreams come true will shoot up dramatically. So open your notebook, pick up your pencil and start reading. Try hard not to think ahead as you read this lesson, just do the exercise in front of you to the best of your ability. And watch what happens.

Lesson Eight:
Practice, Practice,
or How to Throw Yourself a
Dress Rehearsal

Whenever a play or opera is about to open, the company puts on a dress rehearsal—complete with costumes, lights, makeup, full orchestra, and scene changes, all without a public audience. Life, however, rarely gives us the opportunity for this kind of run-through and that's a shame because we could use it. Instead, we're always in a tryout phase when everything's on the line—our contacts, our money, the viability of our dream. While it's great to learn from your mistakes, it sure would be nice if those mistakes didn't cost so much that we can hardly afford to try again.

Well, here's a cheaper, safer way to learn from your mistakes. I want you to have a learning experience that doesn't break your heart or your bankbook—and that *does* try out every skill to go after your big dream that you've learned. Like a mountain climber, you need to know if the ropes will hold. How's your motivation style doing? Are your allies being called on? Do you know what you're feeling? Have you made room in your life for a dream to live? Here's your chance to use everything you learned about resistance and to try out every aspect of the Idea Bank. And to find out how you handle obstacles, disappointments—and success.

You could easily get two additional benefits from doing this dress rehearsal. For one thing, there's a good chance you'll attain a small dream. If your practice goal is to track down family members all over the world, or to build a small boat, or to start your own small theater, you'll get more than practice out of it—you could make that wish come true.

The other benefit? This dress rehearsal will show your hidden dreams that you're willing and able to go the whole distance. That you're ready to be unstoppable. Once they know they can trust you, they'll start to come out of hiding and show you their lovely faces.

That's what Lesson Eight is all about. So put on your costume and warm up your voice. You're about to have a complete run-through.

In this lesson you're going to select a practice wish, one that you're interested in doing but is not your primary heart's desire. Then I'm going to show you some new and enjoyable ways to design a plan. This part of the process can take some time, but I guarantee you'll enjoy every moment. Once you've got the plan in shape, you'll make a list of what needs to be done—and then you'll leave the drawing board and walk out the front door, because it will be time for action. You're going to visit worlds you may never have stepped into before, meet people you wouldn't have met any other way, and learn a surprising amount about the goal you chose—and about yourself.

This probably won't be the first time in this program that you chose an activity you enjoy and lifted it off the paper into real-life action. Back in Lesson Five you did this on a small scale. You took some of those activities you loved as a child and turned them into potent little bits of reality. So, if you left your house and rode a bike for one afternoon, or if you dressed up and went dancing, or drove through the countryside for the first time in a long while, you're ready for this step.

And if you didn't, well, guess what? You're ready anyway. Your future is coming toward you at a rapid pace, and this is one of the few times you'll get a dress rehearsal, so jump in and enjoy it.

Are you sold? Well, just in case, *let me give you some more reasons that practice is a great idea.*

1. You haven't had a chance to try out some planning techniques to see which one works best for you. Your planning style, just like everything else about you, is different from anyone else's. You may be someone who works best with a "to-do" list, or a flowchart; if you've got a great memory and can turn on a dime, you might do your best planning by the seat of your pants. If you haven't developed your own kind of planning methods yet, try mine. They could be just what you're looking for.

2. No matter how many projects you've successfully completed before, everything is different when the goal is only yours. We all carry some baggage along with us when we go after our own dream. It always surprises me how the intensity surges and our responses to problems become complicated when the goal is personal. Joy and fear always get magnified in the process. Bad things feel worse and good ones feel better. You don't want to go through that roller coaster for the first time with a really important wish. It's best to try everything out in advance.

    Just exactly what kinds of complications will you encounter? I don't know. And neither do you. That's the point of practicing.

3. You need to get used to problems. The pursuit of wishes, just like the pursuit of a goal in football, requires

some practice bumping into obstacles. You need to learn how to survive the tackles and get up again when something goes wrong. And something will go wrong. It comes with the territory: you need some information and can't find it, doors get slammed in your face, your friends make fun of you, or some authority tells you your scheme is impossible.

You need to know how it feels to run smack into problems like these. You need to feel frustration and disappointment and abandonment—and all the other feelings that lie in wait, courtesy of the little child inside you—along with the experience of standing up, dusting yourself off and starting again. You want practice dealing with these feelings now, not when the stakes are high.

4. The time has come to bang a big drum, wake up your resistance and say "Come and get me!" If you provoke all the resistance that typically stops you, you'll be able to test yourself against all its moves and try your strategies on it one more time. Keep your notebook handy to log every move your resistance makes, so you can refer to them next time, because resistance loves to make you forget.

5. You can't get too much practice calling on your imaginary allies. I want you to make them a part of your life before you go out into the world to seek your fortune. Going after a dream feels precarious and your survival instincts will weigh you down if you can't create some safety for yourself. Gathering your allies will give you much of the support you need but you need practice calling on them for another reason. To get advice. When you're stumped or uncertain and you ask your allies to answer a question for you, you'll learn to tap your own

subconscious problem-solving abilities. I want you to weave your allies into this practice project until doing so becomes second nature.

6. You need to get accustomed to using your Memory Deck. You've gained so many new insights—about motivation, allies, and feelings, resistance, research—it's impossible to keep them all in your head. After you've had practice, many will become second nature, but how are you supposed to remember them now? The answer is that your Memory Deck stands ready to help you. You've been building it from the beginning and this rehearsal will show you if anything important is missing so you can fix it before you go for your real goal.

Convinced? Okay, let's find the perfect practice goal for you.

Exercise 1: How to Find a Practice Goal

a) Write three imaginary press releases about yourself, set in the future.

A press release, as you may know, is a short announcement sent to the newspapers by people who want to announce an event, like the opening of a store. The writers hope the newspapers will consider their press release interesting enough to print. Typically, a press release is short and has an attention-grabbing headline, like this fictitious one.

Rock Star Buys Tycoon's Yacht.

Joe Shmoe, famous rock star, has bought an enormous yacht from the richest tycoon in the United States.

"I always wanted a really nice boat to sail around in," Joe says, "and my latest platinum record 'Mad for Money' has made it possible." His business manager, Harry Smith, said the yacht cost 20 million dollars and was paid for in cash. "Next, he plans to buy a small country," said Harry. "We're still looking."

I'd like you to write three different kinds of press releases about yourself.

Like my rock star example the first one should be totally fantastic, just to warm you up and remind you to be playful. Think about being a spy, maybe a double agent for a mysterious foreign power. Or be a famous jockey, an explorer of the arctic wastes, or a winner of the state lottery. Because it's so fantastic, you don't need to worry about a time frame, so pretend the event you're describing is happening right now.

Let your fun-loving side take you wherever it likes and have a good time. Most of us immediately limit our wishes with practical considerations before we ever give them a chance to try out their wings. But a press release about an imaginary event allows you to do some bold wishing by eliminating all thought of hard reality from the wishing process. You can say anything you like, so the sky's the limit. That's just the kind of space your imagination needs to really soar. Open your notebook and get to work. When you're finished with this press release you can expect to be smiling.

Now write your second press release. Place this one three months in the future. This is important. If today is January 19, date your press release "April 19" of this year. The event in this release should be a bit more realistic. Write about one that would be a lot of fun, but would require some real planning if you went after it. Here's what a secretary named Kate wrote up in a workshop recently:

Legal Secretary returns from a month collecting songs in Sweden.

Kate L., a legal secretary for a local law firm, has just come back from a month in Sweden, taping and learning to sing folk songs. "My Swedish grandmother used to sing to me when I was very small, and I've always been interested in learning more," she said. What will she do with the songs? "Well, I'm thinking of making a children's record of them, to give to all my nieces and nephews who never knew my grandmother," she said. Record companies take note! This could be a winner!

Here's what Alice, an English teacher wrote:

English Teacher Returns from Geological Expedition to Himalayas.

Alice B., a local high school teacher, just got back from a trip to the "far side" of the Himalayas with a team of geologists studying the source of three of the world's greatest rivers, the Ganges, the Indus and the Brahmaputra. "I'm not a geologist, but they were kind enough to let me tag along. I've always wanted to see the land where these three rivers begin. It was a real thrill," says B. Look for her upcoming article in *The Explorer's Magazine.*

Got it? Now you do it. It may not be easy, but hopefully your first press release, the totally fantastic one, has gotten you warmed up.

As soon as you're finished, I want you to write a third press release, just like the second but with two important differences: this one must be set two years in the future and it must be about the single most wonderful event you can think of. This event doesn't have to look at all possible to you but it must honestly feel completely delightful to imagine. I call this press release "the heart-stopper," because if someone came to your door and offered you the chance to do it, you might faint with joy.

Here are two heart-stopper press releases:

Dave H., a fireman:
Dave H. was just seen far from his home in Des Moines, sitting in a college classroom in Zurich, attending classes of one of the most fascinating professors in the world, Kerzagodzi Mushtanazi. Afterwards, Dave wandered to a coffee shop, read his notes and started to write an essay on philosophy. An hour or so later, five brilliant friends were seen joining him, and they engaged in an animated conversation until the wee hours of the morning.

"I often attend classes in other countries," he said, "wherever I hear of a truly special professor. It's fortunate that I understand most modern and ancient languages."

Nan K., a manager in a utilities company:
Nan K., head of the Nan K. Research Lab in Chicago, has discovered a cure for the common cold. "I'm delighted, of course," she said, "but I'm not at all surprised, because I have always loved medical research. When I opened this research center I knew we'd be making amazing breakthroughs. This is only the beginning."

Those were "heart-stoppers" for the people who wrote them. They tap into very deep wishes, much more so than the second press release. So take some time to think before you write yours. This press release must be about something that would take your breath away if someone offered it to you. (Don't worry, you won't have to do it—yet.)

I'd like you to make this press release longer than the others, as many pages as you can fill. *And then put it away.* I'll ask you to pick it up again later on, but when you're finished with this final press release, the heart-stopper, I think you should take a break.

Go for a walk, do some daydreaming. Give this fantasy some time to float around inside you and lay a few memory tracks in your mind. It's a crucial part of the process.

When you're back, I'll have something unusual for you to do.

Outcome thinking

Now I want to show you a planning and trouble-shooting technique you probably haven't used before.

"Outcome thinking" is a technique developed by political thinkers to help them predict the future. In it, they imagine a possible future event—say landing on the moon or the fall of the Berlin Wall (before either happened, of course)—and then they sit around trying to imagine all the circumstances that would have to happen to cause it. "Humans have landed on the moon," they might say. And then, "How did they get there?" It sounds kind of odd at first, like both ends of the problem are floating in air. But when you use outcome thinking instead of simply setting a goal and planning how to achieve it, you set your sights higher. Because outcome thinking is based on the assumption that anything is possible.

Your press releases all describe imaginary outcomes of this sort. Now I want you to ask yourself the important question: what would it take to make them happen?

b) What would it take to make those imaginary press releases come true?

Use the fantastic press release, the first one you wrote, to practice answering that question. Did you say you flew without an airplane? Then you might need an anti-gravity machine to make it happen. Did you say you ran a fifty-acre ranch full of St. Bernard puppies? Then you might need a rich uncle with a ranch who loved you and dogs. See how it works? Try it out for fun. Let your mind play and enjoy yourself. Then write your answers under the first press release.

When you're finished, you'll have had your first practice session with outcome thinking and you'll be ready to try outcome thinking on your second press release, the more realistic one. Take that press release—the one describing an event that has to be completed in three months—and look at it carefully. Then let your mind become as free as it was in creating the fantastic press release. In your notebook, directly under the second one, write all the things that would have to happen to make it a reality.

Alice B.'s second release was headed, "English Teacher returns from geological expedition to Himalayas."

Here's what Alice wrote:

"I'd have to find some geologists who would let an English teacher tag along on a scientific expedition. I'd have to get a great assistant to stay behind and take care of my home and the mail and other things. I'd have to have plenty of money to pay for that! And I'd have to hire a Jeep to drive me, because I'm not in shape to climb the Himalayas with a bunch of geologists! But Jeeps only go on roads, not all over the place like geologists. So I guess I'd have to have a magic carpet or something that could help me keep up with them."

Can you see how outcome thinking yields high-level creative thinking? You feel much less restrained by reality than if you were writing a "to-do" list or a flowchart. You're forced to be just as concrete, but after all, it's only a fantasy game.

Of course, now you have a list of what would have to happen if you were to attain that second wish—and everything on it looks impossible.

But, look again.

c) The impossible just takes a little longer—stars and zeroes.

Take a look at the list you wrote of what would have to happen for your second press release to come true. The list might have five or ten entries on it.

After each entry I want you to draw either a star or a zero. First, draw a star after every item that you think *you could realistically do without putting your entire life on hold.* When that's done, go back and put a zero next to the entries you don't know how to approach.

Alice: "I looked at my list and I realized that I could actually get an assistant. I'd just have to start asking around. So, I put a star next to that item. Then, I looked at the money entry. How much money would I have to have for such a trip? I'll have to find out. But in the meantime, I could start saving. So I put a star there, too. I don't think I can get a magic carpet so I put a zero after that one."

Now you do it. On your list of what you would have to do to make your press release happen, star the items you can do and put a zero after those you can't. Don't do this exercise in a hurry. Take some time to really think about each item before you label it.

Were you a little surprised, like Alice and Dave, to find out how much of that list you could do? How much you were *already planning to do?* Maybe had even already accomplished? Can you see how far outcome thinking can take you? Now, Alice has by no means decided to go to the Himalayas, and Dave hasn't found a way to go to Switzerland, but both of them are learning to avoid a common trap we all fall into whenever we make a wish.

Impossibility thinking

Most of us treat wishes in a way that's very unfortunate. Almost as soon as we make the wish, we think, "That's impossible," without ever trying it out first. We think that wishful thinking is silly and, as a result, we often drop some very good ideas before giving them a fighting chance.

But wishes aren't intentions, they're just wishes. They can't do any harm, and they don't need to be slapped down as if they could. There's not a reason in the world you shouldn't just play with wishes for the exercise of it, like young animals play to build up their muscles and their timing. When you're watching a cowboy movie you should feel free to think, "Wouldn't it be wonderful to have a horse ranch in Colorado?" even if you don't have the slightest interest in going after such a dream.

Why waste time on such fantasies? Well, if you apply outcome thinking to it, you're not wasting any time at all. *Because outcome thinking turns you from an impossibility thinker into a problem solver.*

If your first thought about any interesting new idea is to think, "Oh, that's impossible, it costs a fortune, I'd have to leave my job . . ." all you've practiced is closing doors. But if you play with an idea by wondering, "What would I have to do to wind up with a horse ranch in Colorado?" then you're practicing inventiveness and problem solving, and having a pleasant fantasy at the same time.

Even if you're certain you don't want to own a horse ranch, you might find yourself arranging to spend a week on a dude ranch in Montana, which might never have occurred to you otherwise. Think about people who lead lives they love: that's the kind of thing they would do!

And if you should come up with some good solutions, but don't want the outcome for yourself, you could save the idea and tuck it away for somebody else. You never know who might need it.

When you start to practice outcome thinking, your way of responding to other people's dreams will also change radically.

Every time you hear someone say something like, "I wish I could play with animals all the time instead of working," or "I wish I could get married," or "I wish I could go to a different high school," you'll stop giving the usual answers we were all trained to give:

"Well, it's not so easy to do these things," or "You'd really have to buckle down and work for it."

As an outcome thinker you will automatically say, "Sounds good. What would have to happen to make that come true?"

When you talk to people that way, you give them a great gift.

You'll be treating their wish with the respect that wishes rarely receive. You'll also be encouraging them to become active in their own problem solving—which may not occur to them otherwise. Most important, you will turn them into outcome thinkers themselves who will, in turn, pass on the same gift to others.

You never know—you could change the world.

d) The pressure cooker interview. Think fast!

"How did you ever get to the Himalayas, Alice B.?" the reporter fired, jamming a mike in her face.

At this moment, I want you to act as if your second press release has appeared in the newspaper and caught the attention of a national news magazine. A reporter has suddenly appeared and is demanding to know how you accomplished your amazing feat. Pick up a pencil and sheet of paper or, even better, speak into a tape recorder, and tell the reporter how you did it.

I know what you're thinking. If you didn't really do it, how can you possibly know *how* you did it?

I'm asking you to ad lib, fake it, get inventive with the truth. After all, if that press release you wrote got published, it would be the first cousin to a lie. And if you had to cover yourself, you'd suddenly have to get very creative. Faking it is a very effective way to come up with answers you don't have.

You think you don't know how? I bet you're wrong. Remember as a child when you got caught doing something you shouldn't? Remember how fast you came up with a tale? Making up stories when you're in trouble is so universal that it's just got to be another one of nature's survival mechanisms. We must have a gene somewhere called "Think fast!"

Here's what Alice wrote for her magazine reporter: "Well, I went to the geology department at a nearby university, where I ran into a graduate student having coffee in the lounge. I asked him if anyone in his department studied the Himalayas and he sent me up to a small office on the third floor, where a woman dressed in khaki fatigues was working with a small rock hammer. She was obviously a geologist. We started talking and I told her my wish and my obstacle. As soon as I got to the part about needing a 'magic conveyance,' she said, 'That's no problem. We use them all the time. We call them ponies.' "

How did Alice come up with that information? She's always loved the Himalayas so she's casually stored away anecdotes she heard through the years. She knew about ponies, she just forgot.

Now you try it. Pretend you're face-to-face with an inquisitive interviewer and answer the question: "How did the event described in your second press release come to pass?" Start writing or speaking into the tape recorder the moment you ask the question. Don't give yourself time to think.

I hope you surprised yourself with the answers you produced. Did you wonder, "Now, where on earth did that come from?" If so, you've just discovered another resource for problem solving that you didn't know you had. Pretending you're being interviewed and having to come up with answers under fire is a high-pressure method of outcome thinking and often yields very good ideas. When you have to come up with answers under pressure, it's amazing how resourceful you can be.

e) *Stars and zeroes again.*

Now, take these ideas you've just come up with, and add them to your list from outcome thinking, the list on which you wrote what would have to happen for your press release to come true. Then mark each of these ideas with a star or a zero using the same thinking as before: can I do it or can't I?

Alice wrote: "Go to the geology department of a university and meet a geologist," and, "Learn how to ride a pony." She wrote stars after both of those entries, because both of them were possible.

Now you do it.

This exercise is a lot of fun, isn't it? But it's more than a game. Your second press release, set three months in the future, could provide the perfect practice goal for your dress rehearsal. After all, you've already come up with some great ideas for how to make it come true!

Exercise 2: *Tune up the Orchestra, the Dress Rehearsal Is About to Begin*

You can pick a different goal and write a new press release, if you like. The practice won't do you a bit of harm. But if at all possible, I'd like you to consider using your second release for this exercise. Let me tell you why.

My experience tells me you probably came up with a bolder idea before you knew I'd ask you to try to really make it happen, and practicing bold ideas is the whole point in a dress rehearsal. Remember, you're warming up so you can go after a life you will love. This is not the time to play it too safe.

The deadline for your practice goal should be far enough away for you to create and execute a detailed plan, but it must be

soon enough to see results within a few months. That time frame
will allow you enough time to practice using every skill you've
learned in the last seven lessons, but still have enough urgency to it
to make everything real—including the excitement of making a
wish come true.

Jane's story will illustrate this better than anything I can say.
Like you, she started with a press release.

Jane's press release:
Single Mother Poet Wins National Award.

Jane Smith won a poet's award and has been given an instructor's job at a summer writing conference, including a house and a
baby-sitter for her children.

"I'm so happy here in the mountains of Montana, I think I'll stay
permanently," the award-winning poet said. "I'm looking for a
school for my kids right now." How will she manage it? "Oh,
they've asked me to teach at this conference forever."

Then Jane asked herself, *What would have to happen to make
that press release come true?*

I'd have to write great poems (she tentatively wrote a star after
this entry), I'd probably have to get a degree from a good college
(zero), I'd need enough money to go to a conference in Montana
(zero), and I'd have to find someone to watch the kids for two
weeks (maybe a star, but probably not).

Jane's magazine interview:

"Well, Miss Reporter, I always knew I'd be a poet someday,
but what made me write award-winning poetry was having kids (!).
At first, I thought that would stop my career dead, and I did stop for
a while. But then one day I was watching the girls talk to each
other and I realized that here was the subject for my poetry: my
children, my hard work, my life. That got me writing again, on
buses, at work, even in front of the TV with the children.

"I went to a local workshop and the instructor recommended a summer conference. That first time, my mother was able to visit and watch the kids for me. I went up to the conference, scared to death, planning to just observe; but at an open reading I couldn't resist reading a poem about my kids. Everyone thought it was wonderful."

Jane continued writing in her notebook journal: "I don't know how I thought of all that! Those were really good ideas!"

Jane added to her first list of stars and zeroes: "Find a poetry journal. Search for a conference next summer. Start saving money for tuition and costs. Ask my mother if she can come take care of the kids. If she can't, maybe I can find a local one or two-day conference for this summer, and next summer try for something bigger. Most of all: *write poetry every day, everywhere I go.*"

She starred every single one of these.

When you do something this wonderful for yourself, it makes you feel like a very valuable human being. Here's what Jane wrote in a letter to me: "I'm so excited to know I'll actually be going to a poetry conference in a few months, even if it's only a small one, near my home. The commitment gets me to keep writing so I can bring something good to show. I'm finally treating myself like I'm somebody special and I swear, it makes me feel like a millionaire!"

Not only did Jane attain a goal she'd never seriously considered before, she now knows how to go after any goal. She's experienced.

And you will be, too, when you use this version of outcome thinking I've designed—with the press release/magazine interview/task list—to create and achieve any kind of delightful practice goal: sign up for a bike trip through Oregon, visit wine country in California, go to the spring fashion show in Milan, make a video presentation for your extended family, or prepare four paintings for your own show! Pick a practice goal that matters to you, save your money, arrange your schedule, talk to other people, borrow a camera or buy a ticket, and in a few months, you're going to be doing it! This dress rehearsal will show you more than anything else how thrilling it is to go after what you want.

And like Jane you'll wake up happiness, love, desire. When that old demon resistance shows up, all that joy will be fresh in your memory and give you the strength to take it on.

Resistance will show up, of course.

What if you get cold feet?

Good. That means everything's right on schedule. Right about now your resistance is getting nervous and saying "Whoa, this is real! She's planning; she's making phone calls; he's at the library; he's looking up things; she's buying plans to build a boat! This is too radical. It must be dangerous!"

What shape will your resistance take? Whatever is most efficient at stopping you.

"I don't have the money for this," "My husband (or wife or family) wants us to take our vacation somewhere else; I'm not a free agent." "I don't deserve to spend this kind of money (or time) on myself." "I'm too old for this." "I'm an outsider; I wouldn't fit in."

You'll recognize your particular brand of resistance every time you go after a goal—and that's exactly what you wanted to know. But you have the opportunity to practice everything you learned in Lesson Six about how to handle it. If you've forgotten, just look in your Memory Deck. You wrote the whole process on one card, just for a time like this.

The awful truth about planning

Thomas à Kempis said, "Man proposes, God disposes."

John Lennon added, "Life is what happens while you're making plans." Experience shows us all that they were right. Plans are pure fiction. There never was one that happened the way it was written down. All the same, planning is a smart thing to do because it gets you into action, and action provides you with many happy accidents. While you're calling people, looking things up at the library, looking through the Yellow Pages, even if you find yourself in one blind alley after another, you're sure to stumble on unexpected opportunity. Stories abound of people walking into the wrong office, or just missing a bus, and encountering someone who changed their lives. Ask anyone how they met their spouses and you'll hear one story after another of unexpected turns. The very unpredictability of life turns into an asset because you don't have to have all the answers, just a general direction and a willingness to show up and see what happens. As Woody Allen said, "80 percent of success is showing up."

When you start planning steps on paper, wishful thinking does an about-face and becomes a to-do list, just as real as grocery shopping. A plan gets you out of your head and into the world, where reality will provide the pieces to your puzzle.

This is the pivotal point of a real transformation. When dreams don't make it to the planning stage, they stay in the clouds, never to become reality. When plans push you into action, however, all kinds of benefits flood into your life. Alone with your dreams you think you have to create everything on your own; out in the world you find much will come to meet you.

Ready to begin? Sure you are.

Let me remind you of the lessons you've learned so far.

You learned in Lesson One how to ignore the kind of thinking that stopped you in the past—the need to be perfect, the self-criticism—and how to design a motivational style that suited you. Remember Popeye's affirmation: I yam what I yam!

You learned how to gather your allies in Lesson Two. They've since given you a feeling of support and access to your own subconscious. Now you've practiced enough to know what makes a good ally and what doesn't so you'll make good choices as you go looking for help.

In Lesson Three, you learned to pay attention to your feelings. Hidden impulses will no longer make you grind to a halt, because you'll recognize them, take care of the underlying feeling, and continue on.

Lesson Four taught you the high price of clutter, how it clogs up not only your home but your mind. With the tricks you learned for clearing it away you have created space for a dream just like this practice one.

Lesson Five showed you that everything you love points to a unique gift within you. It taught you that all loves can turn into wonderful lives.

Lesson Six introduced you to the biggest block in everyone's path toward a dream: resistance. But now you know what it's up to, and how to slip past it.

And Lesson Seven gave you an Idea Bank to help you find any information you need along the way.

And here in Lesson Eight, after one full dress rehearsal you're going to be ready to go for the biggest dream of your life.

All right, curtain's up. You've got all the skills you need. Let the dress rehearsal begin. Pick your goal, look at the entries you starred on your task list and get started working on everything you can. What do you do about the items with a zero after them? Look back into Lesson Seven. You've got everything you need right there to turn those zeros into stars. What do you do about resistance? Don't forget the smallest unit. Now, sit down and make your calls, go out and visit that school, find a local poetry conference and sign up. For the greatest benefit, treat this like a real performance—and let it begin right now.

Win or lose, the longer you stay with this dress rehearsal, the more points you get. Try as hard as you can to push through to the very last scene and make this secondary dream come true. Try not to let anything stop you. But always remember, it's not the outcome that matters here, it's the experience.

And as you step out on the stage before the footlights, remember to congratulate yourself. You've just taken the biggest step so far toward living a life you will love.

LESSON NINE

Build Your Memory Deck/Wish Deck

"Could we know what men are most apt to remember, we might know what they are most apt to do."

MARQUIS OF HALIFAX

◆

"Through loving and hating, all intuition and knowledge of value is built up . . . Applied to the method of scholarship, it means a flair for noticing that certain passages in a text are 'important'—even if it is not yet clear why . . . The individual traits that matter cannot be sought out, they must flash upon the mind."

E. R. CURTIUS, *EUROPEAN LITERATURE AND THE LATIN MIDDLE AGES*

◆

"We encourage you to think wishfully. . . . Once you know what you want, it's easy enough to get it. Once you name a spirit, you have power over it."

PEPPER WHITE, *THE IDEA FACTORY: LEARNING TO THINK AT MIT*

How did your dress rehearsal go? Did you surprise yourself and get all the way to the goal? Did you remember to try out all the things you learned in the first seven chapters? If the answer is yes, congratulations. I'm more surprised than you are. The course of true love rarely runs so smoothly. More likely, you ran into lots of snags. If so, I congratulate you for that, too. That's what practice is for. Now the time has come to sit down and think over what you learned in your dress rehearsal and what you want to do differently next time. You also need to note everything that worked for you, so you won't forget it. Part One of the lesson that follows is about making sure your Memory Deck is complete. It will remind you to put everything you need in it.

Your Memory Deck is going to be a very good friend to you as you head out after the life you love. It will remind you to take care of yourself by using the right kinds of motivation for you. It will help you keep in mind the names of your allies, so you remember you're not alone. It will remind you to check out what you're feeling any time you get confused. Your Memory Deck won't let you forget that you're supposed to keep clearing the decks to make room for the dream that's coming. And it will help to wake you up if resistance has succeeded in putting you in one of those half trances in front of the TV set. Your Memory Deck will keep great research tricks at the tips of your fingers, to jog your memory and help you find what you need.

As you went along you may have written things you wanted to remember on the cards. Before you start on the journey to a life you will love, you might want to go back and make sure you've noted everything that particularly resonated for you. Those notes will give you courage and clarity because they speak directly to you.

They are the tools you need to achieve a dream. Once you've got your Memory Deck in order you're ready to go.

But where do you want to go?

Part Two of this lesson will get you ready to answer that question. You're going to prepare a completely new kind of card deck for this project, called a "Wish Deck." Your colored 3 × 5 index cards are what you'll use to create your Wish Deck. You'll find instructions on how to assemble it in Part Two.

So get ready to complete your Memory Deck and assemble your Wish Deck. You're going to need them both for the final lesson of this book.

Lesson Nine:
Build Your Memory
Deck/Wish Deck

Part 1: Complete Your Memory Deck

You're almost ready to go after the life you love. Your dress rehearsal is over. You found out where you're likely to trip up; you've got a good idea which techniques work best for you, and you've experienced the excitement of the chase. You got some practice pulling out your Memory Deck and looking through it, and you probably found that it isn't quite complete. I've kept you pretty busy in these last eight lessons, so you didn't have much time to work on it, but now is the time to sit down and give it some attention. Your Memory Deck is like your traveling gear. When you climb a mountain, you need to make sure your ropes are in good shape. And when you embark on your journey to a life you love, you need to make sure that your Memory Deck is complete because it could be your most important piece of equipment on this journey. Your Memory Deck was designed by you and it should fit you perfectly. Nothing you need should be missing.

Aphorisms—a personal selection

Out of all the thoughts in this book, I hope you have noted—by highlighting, underlining, or copying—the ones that resonated for you. You may also have gathered some of your own favorites, and put them on a bulletin board or written them in a book. Take them out now and write them on 3 × 5 cards. You need to have those thoughts with you wherever you go. They do something powerful for you and no one entirely understands what that is. But like allies they speak to you in an important way.

Then, whenever you have a free moment—while you're stuck in traffic, or waiting in someone's office, or sitting under a tree—you'll be able to pull out the deck and start looking randomly through the cards. Just glance at them and then put them away. That's all you have to do.

Anything important on those cards will jump out and greet you. On a day that you're not feeling so good about yourself, Popeye's affirmation will show up to say, "I yam what I yam," and give you back your sense of self; or your negative affirmation ("negation") cards with exclamations like "Get me out of here!," "It'll never fly," and "Mom always loved you best" will appear on the top of the deck and make you laugh. When you're waiting for an interview or an audition, your card from Lesson Three, feelings, will be there to get you centered and connected to your emotions. And when you're feeling alone, your allies card will remind you that you have caring friends.

No matter how well you may have learned the lessons in this book, resistance combined with simple memory overload will conspire to make you forget. But with a Memory Deck as traveling equipment, you only need to train yourself to remember to pull it out and look at it a few times a day. The deck will do the rest. Whatever you are ready to see will jump off the card and grab your attention.

Here's what should be in a complete deck:

1. All the cards you've written on so far

Let's review each step in the program to make sure you're "playing with a full deck." Keep a pile of blank cards and your pen or pencil nearby. If you haven't already written cards for each lesson, go back and write them as they come up. Here's what you should have:

From Lesson One, What Motivates You, a card with a list of what keeps you motivated to stay on course. Mine says "Get a buddy to work with," and "arrange a deadline for someone to expect something from me."

From Lesson Two, Gather Your Allies, a card for each of your allies. You might find a photo or drawing of each one and tape it to their card. Or simply write out their names in large clear letters. I copied the cover of the videocassette of the film *Shirley Valentine* for one of mine, and wrote the name "Marco Polo, Traveler" on another.

From Lesson Three, Understand Your Feelings, one card with a list of feelings so you can remember to check which emotions are operating in you at any given time. Add any feelings that aren't already on the list as you experience them.

From Lesson Four, Clear the Decks for Action, some tricks to help you break free of clutter. I have two tricks on my card: "Throw away ten things," and "Don't open junk mail." Someone said she needed to be reminded over and over of her time-clutter problem of taking on too many tasks. Her card says, "Learn to say 'No.'" (Don't write so many tricks on your card that *it* looks cluttered!)

From Lesson Five, Uncover Your Gifts, cards with favorite activities from your past written on them, one to be done every week: "Ride a bike," "Visit the zoo," "Read all afternoon," "Write a poem," etc. (In that lesson I also asked you to invent some careers from those childhood loves and note them on cards. Then I asked you to set them aside. The Wish Deck is where those cards belong. If they're in your Memory Deck, take them out and set them aside for later.)

From Lesson Six, Resistance, a card with the steps to take when resistance makes you drop the ball: "Pick the smallest unit I'm willing to do and fall in love with it. If there is no unit that small, refuse out loud to do anything. Create triggers so I don't forget to keep going. If I realize I've forgotten about the project, start again at once."

From Lesson Seven, The Idea Bank, one card with all the ideas I listed—"wish/obstacle, trade magazines, book indexes, Idea Party, etc." and any good research ideas of your own.

From Lesson Eight, Practice, Practice, Practice, your to-do list from your second press release—with a paper clip on it to remind you throughout the day of what you are supposed to be doing toward achieving your practice goal.

2. The thoughts you want to carry with you

In your deck you should have some cards with the thoughts that were most important to you. One woman's cards included: "Critics are ignorant," "When too many people flunk a program, there's something wrong with the program," and "I need friends who are interesting to me and interested in me." One man wrote, "Clutter is a tribute to indecision," and "Excitement is part happiness and part fear," and "Most people go to their graves with their music still in them." Limit your "thought cards" to five.

Your Memory Deck also needs:

3. Some blank cards to write on

whenever you want to add something to the deck, like sentences that stand out in articles you're reading. I used to cut these out and tape them on my wall, but after a while I stopped looking at them and they became as invisible as wallpaper. Now I put exceptional thoughts or new ideas on an index card and add them to my Memory Deck, because then they'll pop into focus when I need them most. Again, no more than five additional "thought cards." When you add a new card, remove an old one. Don't fool yourself into thinking that a huge pack of good thoughts will do you any good. Your mind can't work with more than ten.

4. A few paper clips attached to a blank card

to indicate especially important cards like your to do list or your most important phone numbers. You can also select a thought that's important for you on a particular day and attach a clip to it. Then, when you take out your deck, you'll automatically be drawn to that card. Be sure not to clip *too* many cards or the signal stops working.

Preparing your Memory Deck can take a while. You might want to do it a bit at a time, so just carry this book with you for a few days so you can page through it and write up new cards whenever you have a free moment.

When your Memory Deck is complete you'll be ready to travel. Then all you need is a destination.

Which brings us to your Wish Deck.

Part 2: Create a Wish Deck

Your Wish Deck is just what it sounds like: a deck of 3 × 5 index cards—preferably in your favorite color—filled with wishes and dreams. What you're going to do now is create some wish cards by writing down the top ten to twenty goals you could be interested in. *The only requirement is that every activity or profession you write on a card stirs a yearning in you.*

Creating a Wish Deck is like gathering together maps of the destinations that most intrigue you, so you can look them over before you decide where you're going. You've already had some delightful daydreams in these pages, and every one of them holds precious information about what will make you happy. You'll be searching through this Wish Deck for that information in the next and final lesson.

When you first start to gather cards, don't leave anything out. Go back through these pages to see which fantasies you enjoyed most. When you're finished, whittle the number of cards down to twenty or less. Gather any ideas for careers or lifestyles that particularly intrigued you. I tried to mention many different kinds of careers and lifestyles for you to look at as you read, just to stir any forgotten talents you might have hidden away. I hope you underlined the ones that woke up feelings in you. Now go back and put these careers and lifestyles on cards, one per card. And look at the pages of fascinating "wish stimulators" at the end of this chapter to help you create a comprehensive Wish Deck. You could end up with dozens of cards, but many will overlap, so do your best to reduce their number to twenty or less. Remember what you learned in Lesson Five: whenever you feel attracted to something, you have a gift for it.

People often say to me, "Throw the whole list in. I want to do everything." That's rarely true—not if you take the time to picture each and every career and think carefully about it. But if you're convinced that you're interested in absolutely everything, then write every single career and lifestyle and fantasy on its own card, carefully and legibly. Just the act of handwriting each individual career or lifestyle on a card will make you think about it enough to check if you really are interested.

And if your interest soars at every single activity, at every career, stop for a moment and consider this delightful prospect: You could easily be a budding free-lance writer, librarian, teacher or speaker, researcher or documentary filmmaker. You have a lot to give the world. If you think that's the case, write down either "free-lance writer," "speaker," "librarian," "teacher," "documentary filmmaker," "researcher"—whichever one of these careers draws you the most.

What is this Wish Deck for? The Heart-stopper.

As of Lesson Nine, you have everything you need to pursue a life you love: motivational tools, allies, an understanding of your feelings, a home that's getting clearer of clutter every day, respect for your gifts, and tricks to protect you from resistance. Not only that, you've been through a full dress rehearsal with a practice goal.

What's the difference between that practice goal and a real goal? Well, a real goal is a heart-stopper.

Possibly the most important card to put in your Wish Deck is the "heart-stopper" from the press release you wrote up in Lesson Seven. Remember it? I called it "the heart-stopper," because if someone came to your door and offered you the chance to do what you wrote, it would take your breath away and your heart would skip a beat.

Take a very careful look at your heart-stopper press release. It just might be the very goal you're looking for. What if it doesn't look possible? That's nothing to be concerned with yet. Later you can throw an Idea Party and find a way to make it work. If you jump right into thinking this wish is impossible, it means your resistance is waking up. Just tell it you're only assembling a Wish Deck, and there's nothing to worry about.

The purpose of the Wish Deck game

Once you've gathered all the interesting goals you can find into a deck of 3 × 5 cards, you're going to play a game that will whittle that deck down to one card.

And that card contains the goal you're going after.

As Mark Twain said, "Put all your eggs in the one basket, *and watch that basket!*" And my mother often confirmed this in her own way. She said, "You can't take one pair of feet to twenty dances."

Wise words. You must make one choice or you'll make none. If that feels restrictive it's because there's something you don't know; when you finally choose a path and go after it, unimaginable opportunities open up to you, opportunities you wouldn't have known about. When you get into action all sorts of new options will come out of hiding, and offer themselves to you. Don't worry, you're not in any danger of picking the wrong goal and getting stuck. Because your choice will come from your own Wish Deck, you're sure to be going in the right general direction.

What if you want more than one goal? Again, not to worry. As you noticed in Lesson Five, you'll have more time than you realize and more goals to pursue.

You'll learn more about this process when you get to Lesson Ten.

In the following pages you'll find some "wish stimulators," a sort of mini-encyclopedia of wishes. They come in all sizes and shapes: I've pulled together true stories and reports from Success Teams, because I so often hear people say, "Oh, I could never do that," whenever they hear of a wonderful and unusual career. These stories tell the real way things happen. They'll make you realize that most things are attainable by normal people like you. And they might show you how to get started on your own dream.

I've also gathered lists of unusual career books to stimulate your wish appetite along with the names of some surprising associations that might stir a long-forgotten interest inside you. Or start a new one.

To stretch your imagination to the limit I couldn't resist throwing in a short list from EarthWatch. EarthWatch is an organization that takes volunteers all over the world to do important work for the ecology and to live fantastic lives at the same time.

Are you ready to go looking for wishes to write on your wish cards? Pick up your pencil and read the following pages. When you find something interesting, write it on a wish card—and remember to write in small print. You'll need plenty of room on these cards for the exercises in Lesson Ten. They're about wonderful people, real people, with lives they love. Some of the stories are from letters I've received, and when you hear someone speak in her own words about how happy she is to garden and write about it in a magazine in Hawaii, you can picture it much better than if you see on a list: "Free-lance writer, specialty gardening."

These people are like you. They're not willing to settle for lives they don't love. So join the club and meet some of the members. Their paths will teach you a lot, and their company might inspire you.

Stories about people who found lives they love

Sometimes all you know is what you don't want.

Gene knew two things: he hated big cities and he loved to fish. He moved to Montana, picking a town that was near the best trout streams. Now, he supports himself with his small construction business and during trout season he knocks off work after lunch to go fishing.

Amy only knew she never wanted to work indoors. Coming from a family of businesspeople, to them she looked as though she was avoiding responsibility. But she became a land surveyor and loved her work. "Whenever I go anywhere in this city, I have an eye for every curve and turn. I know where surveyors stood to lay out every sidewalk or road. I see the beach wall I helped build. It's a world no one but a surveyor sees." She married another surveyor and had two children, one of whom became a forest ranger.

Paula, a chef, had no idea what she wanted, but she knew she didn't want to cook anymore. She took an intensive two year course in photography and plans to become an international food photographer. She has already visited small mountain villages in Central America and photographed the women as they cook. It reminded her that there were aspects of cooking she loved although she never wanted to be a chef again.

Some people decide to follow their noses instead of choosing a goal.

"I'll know what I want when I see it." These words weren't spoken by someone in a department store looking for a blouse, but by some people searching out careers they love—and for them this method works very well.

"It's like playing hide-and-seek," a currency trader told me. "After graduating college I took a job as a stockbroker trainee. I didn't make much money and I was bored on top of it, so I spent some time every day snooping around the other departments.

That's how I discovered currency trading. I found it so much more exciting—and lucrative! But if I hadn't seen people actually trading currency, I never would have thought to go looking for it."

Suzanne took a job as a bookkeeper to make ends meet while, on the side, she got involved as a volunteer, helping a local college bring Russians to visit its business school. Discovering she had excellent organizational and people skills, she started organizing conferences on her own for all kinds of international business exchanges. Presently she's invited to Russia every year to discuss small business with Russian farmers and has helped women start business co-ops in Siberia and Kathmandu!

Some people just need to adjust their course.

Allie, a newspaper reporter, thought she was burned out and started looking for another job. In fact, she loved writing but worked so many hours and was paid so little that she had turned sour on it. She started helping an author edit her book and did such a good job the author's agent asked her to do others. Now she works with several different authors on their manuscripts, earns much more than she was getting before, and loves the work.

Diane loved teaching, standing up in front of people, presenting interesting topics; but she didn't want to teach in a classroom anymore. "I have no idea how to make a career out of teaching any other way!" she said unhappily. Then she found out about the National Speaker's Association. Now she's on the lecture-circuit teaching a course called "Roots: how to write your family's history" making twice her previous salary and working fewer hours. She's in the process of self-publishing a book on her subject to sell wherever she lectures.

Some people do everything *that interests them, one thing at a time.*

Philip studied history, which he loved. Then he moved to Europe for six years, living in a different country every year, visiting all the places he'd read about in his history books, learning the local languages, and supporting himself by teaching English. After a few years, he went to a small island in the Mediterranean and opened a tiny restaurant that was quite successful. The next year he traveled with a band through Eastern Europe, playing guitar and singing. Because of his language skills, he's been offered good positions in European companies but has always preferred to stay independent. He presently tutors students in the United States, and is writing a book of his travels, which he plans to self-publish.

Some people know what they love but can't figure out how to make a living at it.

Jeannie worked for a bookstore and initiated a system of taking books to conferences and selling them at a table in the lobby. She loved making wonderful books available to people who wouldn't otherwise know about them. But her employer wasn't as enamored of the idea and made her stop. So Jeannie called other bookstores and told them what she wanted to do. A number of them offered her a job on the spot. She's negotiating for a part-time position so she can start her own business on the side, traveling from one small independent bookstore to another, teaching the owners the merchandising skills she's developed. Her on-line name is Bookgenie, and it fits.

Some people only know where *they want to live, but can't figure out how to make a living once they get there.*

Bella: "I wanted to live overseas but could never find a job once I got there, so I came back to the states and just became a banquet waitress in a hotel because I was too disappointed to do anything else. After a while I moved into the banquet sales department and discovered that's how hotels make much of their money! I love talking to people, and I brought in lots of conferences. They liked what I did so much they sent me to one of their hotels in Hong Kong and made me sales manager! Now I meet a completely international crowd and I go to Nepal and India on the weekends!

With my experience I think I can get a job like this almost anywhere."

Sometimes all you want is to be your own boss.

Magazines like *Home Office Computing, Inc.,* and *Entrepreneur* are full of fascinating stories of people who made it on their own in dozens of different ways. For more great stories about how some entrepreneurs actually got started read one of my favorite books, *The Woman's Guide to Starting a Business,* by Claudia Jessup and Genie Chipps, Holt & Co. My edition says 1991, but they update every few years.

In their pages, they interview a woman who started a bookstore specializing in murder mysteries, another who created a successful art gallery in Santa Fe, one whose business helps families relocate to Chicago, still another who has her own talent agency in Minneapolis, a saleswoman who started a business carrying high-tech medical services in mobile units to rural hospitals in Virginia, someone else who created a traveling lunch counter bringing food to people in offices—and many, many more. All these people decided to live life on their own terms, and their stories will inspire you.

Some people have wishes that seem impossible:

JC: "I am a legal secretary from New England who has always hated pushing paper while all I've ever wanted is to work with dolphins. I didn't know why or how to do it. My husband and kids are settled in so I figured we couldn't move anyway. Then I started using your wish/obstacle solution. I just told everybody what I wanted and I didn't care if they thought I was crazy. Someone directed me to an organization called 'Dolphins Plus' and they told me about a six-day course at the Marine Mammal Research and Education Center in the Florida Keys—and guess what? I'm going there this summer to take the course! I also got referred to the National Wildlife Federation's new program in Orlando called NatureLink. It enables people to become active environmental stewards by teaching them how to protect dolphins, manatees, sea turtles, and other endangered marine species through beach and stream cleanups.

"I am on my way to being the most happy person in the world. I have asked my husband to come with me and photograph the dolphins while I interact with them and he's happy to give it a try. My kids are ready to move to Florida!

"Thank you for your work. Without it, I probably would still be thinking that pushing paper was the right thing for me."

Reports from Success Teams

I don't keep track of the Success Teams around the world; there must be hundreds. But I do get wonderful letters almost every day. Here are some that might inspire a few ideas for you.

D.B.: "My dream was to live in Hawaii and write for a garden magazine, so my Success Team convinced me to go to Wiamaya Falls, Hawaii, for two months just to see if I liked it. I got a sabbatical from my job and went to Hawaii, where I walked into a local plant nursery and struck up a conversation with the owner, an ornamental horticulturist. We hit it off right away and he rented me a beautiful cottage on the beach. I went in to help him out every day, just because I love plants, and then he hired me. Now I walk three miles to work every day on the most beautiful road you ever saw and I just finished my first article for a local garden newsletter."

Ellie L.: "I'm a forty-seven year old, happily married housewife with a part-time job, who always secretly longed to be a torch singer. At the insistance of a wonderful Success Team I put together, I took lessons for several months and then made my first appearance at open-mike night in a big nightclub in Hollywood. What happened was amazing. My friends found out and came from all over the country to see me; they called each other and had such a big surprise for me, there were even people I know from kindergarten, dressed in tuxedos, and arriving in limousines. To be honest, I was terrified up on that stage, but I saw them all smiling at me, and I just loved it. Look what you can get if you're willing to risk a little on a dream." She now sings regularly in the L.A. area.

K.R.: "I had two dreams when I went to your workshop last year: I wanted to travel and I wanted to promote the San Francisco Girls' Chorus. After getting into a team, I got so much support that I came up with a plan to ride my bike across the United States to promote the chorus. And I did it!"

Elizabeth P.: "I'm in my sixties and my Success Team is doing great. I've realized my dream of going into the theater and I just completed a role in a play called *Octette Bridge Club.* My team-mate V.V. (who never finished college) is now in her second year of a master's degree in social work. J.L., the artist/poet, is finally going to school full time to study music, art, and literature (the life's dream she thought she wasn't allowed to have)."

Albert R.: "One member of the team became a flight attendant, her lifelong dream. One started out taking pictures of homes that were for sale, and wound up getting her real estate license and becoming the number one salesperson in her office. Another traveled with a video camera and has sold tapes to a TV travel channel. One, who loves eating, became a local food critic and now eats for free! One broke into local TV with her own show, and conducts training workshops for corporate employees about managing finances. It's been astonishing!"

Anne P.: "I recently came back from a fabulous summer camp where I worked as a Film and Photography Specialist. I got the job as a result of working your techniques. I'm writing you so other people will understand that there is a way to do this."

Kelley S.: "I'm now a chiropractor in upstate New York, after leaving my job as a social worker in New York City and going to school. I now live in paradise on my own land. I'm on the city board and feel that I'm an important part of my community."

Ruth S.: an accomplished cellist in her forties, found it impossible to get work. Then she started the Festival Chamber Music Society and has been getting rave reviews ever since. She sent me this *New York Times* review: "The most impressive element of The Festival Chamber society is its roster of participating artists—master players all!"

Brian S.: "About a year ago I had a dream to become a comedy writer and performer, but just couldn't find the nerve to go up on stage. Quite frankly, I needed a miracle. As fate would have it I found a copy of *Wishcraft* in a bookstore. The stories of people and their problems and successes were something I really related to. I put an ad in a weekly paper looking for a team and found four great people willing to join a team.

"Through the team, I got in touch with someone who ran classes on stand-up comedy, with the graduation being a performance in front of an audience. I did a seven-minute act in front of more than 200 people who actually laughed and thought I was funny! And after I got off stage, my team was there for hugs and handshakes! Now I realize I needed people to listen to my act, to help me narrow down tons of material, and to be there for support when I finished!"

L.S.: "Recently I discovered some writing I did in a team back in the early 80s when I lived in Colorado. I was shocked to see how close the dream I only dreamed of then is to my present reality!" (Enclosed: article from *Las Cruces Sun-News* with photo of L.S. in front of her painting at an art show.)

Lisa M.: "I had no idea where to start, even where I wanted to go. I only knew I loved gorillas, and you persuaded me to learn everything I could and get involved with the Gorilla Foundation. Everybody told me I was foolish and I was afraid they might be right, but now I work with gorillas every day in one of the biggest zoos in America! I've been to Borneo twice working with the apes, and I've even helped raise baby gorillas."

K.T.: "I turned off the critics inside my head, and created a support team for myself. Now my products for children are in three major catalogs, and I'm designing new ones all the time."

T.W.: "I desperately wanted to live in Italy. I speak Italian, I love to study. But I have an MBA and felt obliged to come back to the states and use it. Through your 'Live a Life You Love' tapes, I set up Idea Parties and got great advice and connections. Now I'm building a program to teach young Italian women how to start their own businesses! I'm going to take it to Italy next year!"

K.N.: "I'm an actress, but I wanted to direct and I didn't want to live in New York. I'm now working on getting a grant to start a nonprofit regional theater for at-risk kids in my home town of Kansas City."

B.Z.: "My dream was to help stop violence. I just didn't know where to begin. I belonged to lots of organizations, but didn't feel I was making a difference. Now I have developed a presentation, and I'm taking it to all the local schools. It's full of games and simulations, and the kids really seem to listen to it!"

V.M.: "I was embarrassed to admit it, because I have a great job and I've always been independent, but I wanted to find a good man and get married. I felt like admitting that would make me look desperate and stupid, but you taught me to respect every wish, and made me see that I had the right to go after what I needed without ever feeling ashamed. Now I'm joining organizations and meeting some wonderful guys. My friends keep finding available men and having us over for dinner. They never did that before—because I never asked them to."

Which brings us to people who need both love and work.

The last story is one of my favorites. It's about Lila, who came from a Czechoslovakian family. Though all her family wanted was for her to go to college, Lila dreamed of traveling the world, and after two semesters of college, she quit and went to school to become a secretary. Lila figured she'd have to marry and settle down to a conventional life one day, so for five years she traveled all over the world on month-long trips, working as a secretary in between to save up money. Soon, Lila's happiness inspired her family and, for the first time, they started traveling for pleasure, too. One day her father said, "I'd like to see Alaska. Would you like to come with me?" Since she was almost twenty-seven and figured she'd have to settle down soon, Lila was delighted, and joined him on what she thought would be her farewell trip.

The trip was led by a lecturer named Bob.

Bob also had an unusual life. He was a very bright kid, but he'd hated school because it bored him to death. The only thing that had interested him was a scuba diving class he was able to take instead of physical education. Finally, he dropped out of high school, took an equivalency exam and went to work at a fast-food chain store. Within a few months, he became the manager, and by the time he turned eighteen, he was making sixty thousand dollars a year.

Then one day he walked out.

"I just knew in my heart that a nine-to-five job would kill me." Bob moved to San Diego and taught scuba diving in the mornings. He spent his afternoons at the aquarium at the Scripps Institute of Oceanography, visiting with the people who worked there.

"This was more exciting to me than anything I would ever learn in college, so I volunteered to help them collect unusual fish for the aquarium and eventually they hired me as a fish collector. I didn't even know a job like that existed! They started getting me involved in long-distance fish-collecting trips to the South Sea Islands and the Marquesas, and eventually I went around the world on a collecting expedition for them.

"One day, a cruise ship owner I'd met in my travels asked me to guide a tour to the arctic for a few weeks. I got a leave of absence from Scripps and went to Alaska."

Bob was the tour instructor on Lila's ship. They fell in love, married and have been together for ten years. When they're not out sailing, they have a mail-order business, which they run together. Bob doesn't work a nine-to-five job and Lila has never had to settle down.

There you are. A sampling of stories about real people who have found a way to live lives they love. I hope it's taken some of the mystery away, and allowed you to start believing, "I could do that!" Think about what you've just read and see if it stimulates any thoughts of something you might love. If so, write a wish card for the ideas that attract you the most.

Here are some book titles to give you more ideas

I have no idea what's between the covers of most of these books, but my impulse is to recommend them sight unseen because I have a special feeling for people who help us move outside our own experience into their world. I got these names from a bookstore called Amazon.com on the Internet. If you are on the "Net," you can find them at http://www.amazon.com. Others are from the *Solo Sourcebook* by Teri Lonier, in most bookstores. A few I've included are from my own bookshelf.

Animals
Management of Crocodiles in Captivity
(FAO Conservation Guides, No 22)
by Melvin Bolton
Food & Agric Org, 1990

Opportunities in Animal and Pet Care Careers
by Mary Price Lee, Richard S. Lee
Vgm Career Horizons, 1990

**The Intelligence of Dogs: Canine
Consciousness and Capabilities**
by Stanley Coren
Macmillan, 1994

**How to Get Your Pet into Show
Business**
by Arthur J. Haggerty
Howell Book House Inc., 1994

**Well Trained Llama: A Trainers
Guide**
by Betty Barkman, Paul Barkman
Birch Bark Pr., 1989

Goat Farming
by Alan Mowlem
Diamond Farm Book Publishers,
1992

**Organization and Management of
a K-9 Therapy Group**
by Jacqueline P. Root
Denlingers Pub. Ltd, 1990

Koko's Story
(about Koko, the gorilla)
by Francine Patterson, Ronald H.
Cohn
Scholastic Paperbacks Trade, 1988

**Raising Gordy Gorilla at the San
Diego Zoo** (Zoo World)
by Georgeanne Irvine
Simon & Schuster Juvenile, 1993

Art
Gallery Management
by Rebecca Zelermyer
Syracuse U. Pr., 1976

**Jobs in the Arts and Arts
Administration**
by J. Jeffri
Ctr. Arts Info., 1981

**Marketing Your Arts & Crafts:
Creative Ways to Profit from
Your Work**
by Janice West
Summit Group, 1994

**The Career Cartoonist: A Step-By-
Step Guide to Presenting and Selling
Your Artwork**
by Dick Gautier
Perigee, 1992

**The Complete Photography Careers
Handbook**
by George Gilbert
Consultant Pr., 1992

Entrepreneuring
**Kitchen Table Publisher:
The Master Manual:
How to Start, Manage and Profit
from Your Own Independent
Publishing Company**
By Thomas A. Williams
Venture Publisher, 1994

How to Get Fabulously Rich
by Thomas Rockwell, Anne Canevari
Green
Dell Pub. Co., 1991

**Entrepreneuring: A Nurse's Guide to
Starting a Business**
by Gerry Vogel, Nancy Doleysh
Natl. League Nursing, 1994

A Teen's Guide to Business
by Linda Menzies, Oren S. Jenkins, &
Rickell R. Fisher,
MasterMedia Limited, 1992
Written by three teenage
entrepreneurs, action-oriented guide
with tips and quizzes. Role models
from all ethnic, economic, and
geographic backgrounds, extensive
resource list.

Better Than a Lemonade Stand!
by Daryl Bernstein,
Beyond Words Publishing, Inc., 1992
Written by a 15-year-old
entrepreneur (with seven years of
business experience!), this book
presents 51 easy-to-launch small
businesses that require little or no
start-up costs and are ideally suited
for youthful entrepreneurs.

**Advertising Career Directory: A
Practical One-Stop Guide to Getting
a Job in Advertising**
by Bradley J. Morgan (Editor)
Published by Visible Ink Pub., 1992

**Garage Sale and Flea Market
Annual: Cashing in on Today's
Lucrative Collectibles Market**
Collector Books, 1995

**The Bbs Construction Kit: All the
Software and Expert Advice You
Need to Start Your Own Bbs**
by David Wolfe
Wiley John & Sons Computer, 1994

**How to Start and Run Your Own
Advertising Agency**
by Allan Krieff
McGraw Hill, 1993

**How to Start Your Own
Appliance Repair Business from
Home, Without Capital or
Experience:** For Major Appliances
by Rey D. Longhurst
Longhurst Rey, 1988

**Start Your Own Information
Brokerage**
by Susan Rachmeler
Pfeiffer & Co., 1995

**Make Money Reading Books!:
How to Start and Operate Your
Own Home-Based Freelance
Reading Service**
by Bruce Fife
Piccadilly Books, 1993

**The 10 Hottest Consulting
Practices: What They Are, How
to Get into Them**
by Ron Tepper
Wiley John & Sons Trade
Publication date: May 1995
ISBN: 0471110000

**How to Start and Operate Your
Own Bed-And-Breakfast/Down-To-
Earth Advice from an Award-
Winning B&B owner**
by Martha Watson Murphy, Amelia
Rockwell Seton (Illustrator)
Owlet, 1994

**How to Open and Operate a
Home-Based Catering Business**
by Denise Vivaldo
Globe Pequot Pr., 1993

Start Your Own At-Home Child Care Business
by Patricia C. Gallagher
Young Sparrow Pr., 1994

Start Your Own Coffee & Tea Store
by Joann Padgett
Pfeiffer & Co., 1994

How to Make $20,000 a Year in Antiques and Collectibles Without Leaving Your Job
by Bruce E. Johnson
Ballantine Books Inc., 1992

Farming, Gardening
Art of Natural Farming and Gardening
by Ralph Engelken
Barrington Hall Press, 1981

How to Find a Good Job Working With Plants, Trees, and Flowers: Earn Income and Enjoy Life
by Francis X. Jozwik
Andmar Pr., 1993

Backyard Market Gardening: The Entrepreneur's Guide to Selling What You Grow
by Andrew W. Lee
Good Earth Pub., 1995

Beginning Farming and What Makes a Sheep Tick
by Lowell T. Christ Ensen
Pinon Press, 1994

Commercial Catfish Farming
by Jasper S. Lee
Interstate Printers & Pubs Inc., 1991

Crustacean Farming
by D. O'C. Lee, J. F. Wickins
Halsted Press, 1992

Earthworms for Ecology and Profit: Scientific Earthworm Farming
by Ronald E. Gaddie, Donald E. Douglas
Bookworm Pub. Co., 1976

Family Farming: A New Economic Vision
by Marty Strange
U. Nebraska Press, 1989

Grow It: The Beginner's Complete In-Harmony-With-Nature Small Farm Guide: From Vegetable and Grain Growing to Livestock Care
by Richard W. Langer, Susan McNeil (Illustrator)
Noonday Press, 1994

Fashion (Career Portraits)
by Lucia Mauro
Ntc Pub Group, 1995

Green Careers
Environmental Career Directory: A Practical, One-Stop Guide to Getting a Job Preserving the Environment
by Bradley J. Morgan, Joseph M. Palmisano, Diane M. Sawinski (Editors)
Visible Ink Pub., 1993

Helping Others
150 Careers in the Health Care Field
by Janice Eldredge (Compiler), Darrell Buono (Editor)
US Dir. Serv., 1993

How to Successfully Start a
Grassroots Non-Profit
Organization
by Darryl R. Webster
Achievement USA Corp., 1993

Love
Haven't You Been Single Long
Enough?
A Practical Guide for Men or
Women Who Want to Get Married
by Milton Fisher
Wildcat Pub., 1992

How to Get Married One Year
from Today: Advice on Romance
for Men and Women
by Martin V. Gallatin
Spi Books, 1994

Performing Arts
Inside the Music Business
by Tony Barrow, Julian Newby
Chapman & Hall, 1995

Plays, Players, and Playing: How
to Start Your Own Children's
Theater Company
by Judith A. Hackbarth
Piccadilly Books, 1994

Successful Stand-Up Comedy
by Gene Perret
Samuel French Trade, 1994

Club Date Musicians: Playing the
New York Party Circuit (Music in
American Life)
by Bruce A. MacLeod
U. Illinois Press, 1993

Take It from the Top! How to Earn
Your Living in Radio & T.V. Voice-
Overs
by Alice Whitfield
Ring U. Turkey Press, 1993

Making It in Broadcasting: An
Insider's Guide to Career
Opportunities
by Leonard Mogel
Collier Books, 1994

How to Launch Your Career in TV
News
by Jeff Leshay
Vgm Career Horizons, 1993

You Oughta Be Me: How to Be a
Lounge Singer and Live Like One
by Bud E. Luv
St. Martins Pr. Paper, 1993

Stage Design and Properties
(Schirmer Books Theatre Manuals)
by Michael Holt
Schirmer Books, 1991

Photographer's Market:
Where & How to Sell Your
Photographs
by Michael Willins (Editor)
Writers Digest Books, 1994

Songwriter's Market:
Where & How to Market Your Songs
by Cindy Laufenberg (Editor)
Writers Digest Books, 1994

Poet's Market: Where &
How to Publish Your Poetry
by Christine Martin (Editor)
Writers Digest Books, 1994

Artist's & Graphic Designer's Market:
Where & How to Sell Your Illustration, Fine Art, Graphic Design & Cartoons
by Mary Cox (Editor)
Writers Digest Books, 1994

Writer's Market: Where & How to Sell What You Write
by Mark Garvey (Editor)
Writers Digest Books, 1994

Dancing . . . for a Living
by Don Mirault
Rafter Pub., 1994

Acting and Directing
by Russell J. Grandstaff
Passport Books, 1989

The Audition Book: Winning Strategies for Breaking into Theater, Film, and Television
by Ed Hooks
Back Stage Books, 1989

Creating Special Effects for TV and Film
by Bernard Wilkie
Hastings House Pub., 1977

Grande Illusions: A Learn-By-Example Guide to the Art and Technique of Special Make-Up Effects from the Films of Tom Savini
by Tom Savini
Pub. Group West, 1983

Stay Home and Star!: A Step-By-Step Guide to Starting Your Regional Acting Career in Commercials, Industrials, Theatre, Movies, Print, Modeling
by William Paul Steele
Heinemann, 1991

Make Your Own . . . : Videos, Commercials, Radio Shows, Special Effects, and More
Ellen Sasaki (Illustrator)
Price Stern Sloan Pub., 1992

How to Be a Male Go Go Dancer and Get Rich
by Ray Costa
Costa, 1985

Hit Me With Music: How to Start, Manage, Record, and Perform With Your Own Rock Band
by Stephanie Powell
Millbrook Press, 1994

Cartoon Animation: Introduction to a Career
by Milton Gray
Samuel French Trade, 1991

Travel
Jobs for People Who Love to Travel: Opportunities at Home and Abroad
by Ronald L. Krannich Ph.D., Caryl Rae, Ph.D., Krannich Impact Pubns, 1995

Careers for Travel Buffs and Other Restless Types (Vgm Careers for You Series)
Vgm Career Horizons, 1991

Choosing an Airline Career: In-Depth Descriptions of Entry-Level Positions, Travel Benefits, How to Apply and Interview
Capri Pub., 1993

Handbook of Offshore Cruising: The Dream and Reality of Modern Ocean Sailing
by Jim Howard
Sheridan House, 1994

Miscellaneous Careers
Be Your Own Headhunter Online: Get the Job You Want Using the Information Superhighway
by Pam Dixon, Sylvia Tiersten
Random House Electronic Pub., 1995

Becoming a Manager: Mastery of a New Identity
by Linda A. Hill
Harvard Bus. Sch. Pr., 1992

Book Publishing Career Directory: A Practical, One-Step Guide to Getting a Job in Book Publishing
(Vip Career Advisor Series)
by Bradley J. Morgan, Joseph M. Palmisano (Editor)
Visible Ink Press, 1992

Careers for Bookworms & Other Literary Types (Vgm Careers for You)
by Marjorie Eberts, Margaret Gisler
Vgm Career Horizons, 1995

Getting into Advertising/a Career Guide
by David Laskin
Ballantine Books Trd. Pap., 1986

How to Get a Job in Sports: The Guide to Finding the Right Sports Career
by John Taylor
Collier Books, 1992

I Could Do Anything If I Only Knew What It Was: How to Discover What You Really Want and How to Get It
by Barbara Sher
Delacorte Press, 1995

Law Enforcement Careers: A Complete Guide from Application to Employment
by Ron Stern
Lawman Pr., 1988

Life Outside the Law Firm: Non-Traditional Careers for Paralegals
by Karen Treffinger
Delmar Pub. Inc., 1995

My First Year As a Lawyer: Real-World Stories from America's Lawyers
by Mark Simenhoff (Editor)
Walker & Co, 1994
ISBN: 0802774172

Newspapers Career Directory: A Practical, One-Stop Guide to Getting a Job in Newspaper Publishing
by Bradley J. Morgan (Editor)
Gale Research, 1993

The No-Nonsense Guide to Computing Careers
by Mark Rettig
Assn. Computing Machinery, 1992

So You Want to Be a Doctor
by Stuart C. Zeman
10 Speed Press, 1992

Temp by Choice
by Diane Thrailkill
Career Pr. Inc., 1994

Selling: The Mother of All Enterprise
by William H. Blades,
Marketing Methods Press, 1994

Miscellaneous books from my bookshelf

Because I happen to think that "dilettante" is a word of praise and a very fine lifestyle, here's my own short list for all you would-be philosophers, historians, linguists, geographers, and lovers of the life of the mind.

Pythagoras' Trousers: God, Physics, and the Gender Wars
Margaret Wertheim
Random House, 1995

Water, Ice & Stone Science and Memory on the Antarctic Lakes
Bill Green
Harmony Books, NY, 1995

Dirt: The Ecstatic Skin of the Earth
William Bryant Logan
G. P. Putnam Sons, 1995

The Moral Animal: Why We Are The Way We Are: The New Science of Evolutionary Psychology
Robert Wright
Random House, 1994

The Art of Mathematics
Jerry P. King
Ballantine Books, 1992

Emblems of Mind: The Inner Life of Music and Mathematics
Edward Rothstein
Random House, 1995

Harm de Blij's Geography Book
Harm de Blij
John Wiley and Sons, 1995

Four Thousand Years Ago
by Geoffrey Bibby
Alfred Knopf, 1962

The Mirror of Language: A Study in the Medieval Theory of Knowledge
Marcia Colish
University of Nebraska Press, 1968

The Slayers of Moses: The Emergence of Rabbinic Interpretation in Modern Literary Theory
by Susan A. Handelman
State University of New York Press, Albany, 1982

Associations

Organized Obsessions(!)

This is actually a book, a collection of 1,001 offbeat and quirky associations, fan clubs, microsocieties, and other organizations you can join, so I put it here with associations. I'm including their phone (800) 776-6265 and fax number (800) 776-6265 because you won't find it in the Encyclopedia of Associations.

To contact any of the following groups, check the *Encyclopedia of Associations.*

American Association of Hypnotherapists
American Association of Woodturners
American Folklore Society
American Holistic Health Association
American Society of Furniture Artists
Artist-Blacksmith's Association of North America
Association of Bridal Consultants
Cake, Candy & Party Supply Association
Children's Book Writers
Clowns of America International
Comedy Writers Association
Embroiders' Guild of America
Garden Writers Association
Glass Art Society
Golf Course Builders Association
Handweavers Guild of America
Industrial Designers Society

Institute of Diving
Institute of Store Planners
International Association Fitness Professionals
International Brotherhood of Magicians
International Sculpture Center
International Window Cleaning Association
Interpreters for the Deaf
Keyboard Teachers Association
Lighting Management Company
Midwives Alliance/N. America
National Blacksmiths & Welders
National Chimney Sweep Guild
Society of North American Goldsmiths
Songwriters Guild of America
Teachers to Speakers
Toy Library Association

Earthwatch has the following volunteer opportunities and available briefings. To contact them, call 1-800-776-0188 x118. I include this list just to make you realize what a lot of average people are getting involved in. (When I made my Wish Deck I had to restrain myself from writing every one of these down!)

Aborigines, Australia
Ancient Mallorca
Archeology, Arctic Canada
Archeology, Tennessee
Architecture, Finland
Barrier Reef, Belize
Bears, North Carolina
Black Rhino, Zimbawe
Blue Holes, Bahamas
Bluecrabs, Virginia
Butterflies, Ecuador
Castles, France
Caves, Oregon
Coral Reefs, Fiji
Crocodiles, South Africa
Dinosaurs, Argentina
Dolphins, Monterey, CA
Drums of Senegal
Eagles, Scotland
Elephants, Botswana
Farming, China
Festivals, India
Fish, Amazon
Folklore, Tanzania
Forest Bison, Thailand
Fossil Elephants, China
Fossil Rain Forest, Australia
Geoarcheology, Greece
Giant Clams, Great Barrier Reef
Glaciers, Norway
Himalayan Geology, India
Incas, Chile

Lemon Sharks, Bimini
Manatees, Florida
Marine Flora, Azores
Maya Culture, Guatamala
Migratory Birds, Alaska
Monkeys, Sri Lanka
Mountain Lions, Utah
Muskoxen, Alaska
Neanderthal, Spain
Old Growth Forest, Ontario
Orca, Washington
Preserving Art, Venice
Pueblo, Arizona
Rain Forest, Borneo
Restoring Wetlands, Nepal
River Dolphins, China
Rivers, Estonia
Rock Art, Utah
Roman Farm, Italy
Scythian Archeology, Russia
Sea Level Rise, Trinidad
Sea Turtles, Brazil
Seals, Santa Cruz, CA
Shipwreck, Caribbean
Solar Ovens, Kenya
Songbirds, Hungary & Italy
Volcanos, Kamchatka, Russia
Whales, Hawaii
Whaling Village, Alaska
Wildflowers, Colorado
Wolves, Poland

That's the list.

Now you've read the stories, scanned the book titles and associations and this amazing list. Did it send your imagination whizzing in all directions? That's what I was hoping. Do you want to write more wishes than anyone could possibly fit into one life? Good. That was part of the plan. I want you to be awake to what a rich place this world is, and how many opportunities are out there for you.

Now, look at every item that woke up feelings of interest or longing. Select up to twenty favorites and write each one at the top of a card.

Now be prepared to play the card game of your life!

LESSON TEN

Live the Life You Love

"The vitality of thought is in adventure. Ideas won't keep. Something must be done about them."

ALFRED NORTH WHITEHEAD

✦

"He that leaveth nothing to chance will do few things ill, but he will do very few things."

MARQUIS OF HALIFAX

✦

"Play is work a body is not obliged to do."

MARK TWAIN

✦

"Business is really more agreeable than pleasure; it interests the whole mind, the aggregate nature of man, more continuously and more deeply. But it does not look as if it did."

WALTER BAGEHOT

To live the life you love, you must do what you love. And you can't choose what you love, you can only discover it.

Why do you suppose you love dancing so much and your best friend doesn't? How can you find the words to explain how fantastic it is to move your body to music?

You can't. We're so different from each other that explaining why you love what you love to someone else is like trying to explain opera to a cat. And how many times have you tried to care about something you didn't love? I don't know how many sports events I've attended, drawn by the shine in someone else's eyes, only to sit there bored because I didn't have the senses to see what they saw.

So what is behind the strange pull of what you love? Where does it come from? Everything points to one answer: it's the magnetism of your gifts and your talent. The attraction you feel was put there to make you go toward the activities you'd be best at. Nature seems to believe that if you go with your strengths, it will be good for your survival and the survival of your people. That's got to be what makes us love success and satisfaction, too. Nature makes them feel good so they will attract us.

If all this seems painfully obvious, then why isn't everyone living by this understanding? Look around at how few people really do what they love—by my definition that also means what makes them happy, what they're brilliant at, what they're proud of. Then look at how many people are doing work they don't like at all—don't give their best, and aren't proud of.

For your sake and the sake of the world, you must follow your gifts.

One question is—where do they lead? The other is—when will you go after them?

Lesson Ten:
Live the Life You Love

Every single choice you made in assembling your Wish Deck was enormously significant. Each career you wrote on a card stirred something deep within you in a way no one understands completely. Not even you. This pull is as natural as those of hunger, sexuality, or the love of your babies—and it's trying to tell you something.

So if you listen, you'll find exactly what you need to know to live a life you love.

Being drawn to something is the first step. It puts you in the right ballpark. But uncovering *why* you are drawn to it can be tricky. If you decided, for example, to base a career on your love of animals, the first thing you might think is that you should become a veterinarian. (Many people do exactly that!) If your heart goes cold at that thought, however, you could easily become confused and back away entirely from working with animals. *That would be a terrible mistake.* Because you might be a genius dog breeder or trainer, or brilliant at studying the habits of animals in the wild, or gifted as a free-lance writer who specializes in animals of the rain forests or as a scholar who discovers how animals migrated through the continents during the Ice Age. You could even work with an airport, protecting birds from airplanes—and vice versa. You could be a sheepherder in New Zealand. You could be a photographer of eagles.

Whenever you love something, you absolutely must move in

close and take a careful look at it. Something in there is calling to you, and you've got to pay attention.

Until you know why *you love something, you can't follow it—and you can't abandon it either.*

That's what the exercises in this lesson are for. They will transform the cards in your Wish Deck into a map of your gifts. They'll make you see why you're drawn to the things you love so you can choose the right path for you.

But, before you begin, just sit back and take a cool look at your Wish Deck. That's an amazing pile of 3 × 5 cards you've assembled. You understand, don't you, that *no one else will ever have a Wish Deck exactly like yours.* You assembled it from stirrings within your soul and it reflects how complex, rich, and original you are. These cards hold a secret for you, *only* for you, and they're going to help you zero in on the source of the mysterious magnetism that made you create them.

There are nine steps to reducing your Wish Deck down to the one right card. If it doesn't suit your personal style to go through the whole process, skip the first eight steps and go directly to step nine.

Now, clear a lot of space on a table, get some pens and pencils ready and set your Wish Deck before you. You don't have to do any writing yet. The first exercise is just going to help you sort the cards into different piles. Start by asking yourself the following question:

Step 1: How would I wish to take each of these activities all the way to the top?

Remember Lesson Five: "Uncover Your Gifts"? You looked at three periods in your past—childhood, adolescence and young adulthood—and listed everything you loved at that time. Then you imagined that you took each one of those loves to the limit, as far as it would go. If you liked bike riding, you imagined that you were a champion racer, or the builder of the best bike in the world. If you liked being outdoors, you imagined you were an explorer or a world famous mountain climber.

Most of those beloved activities from Lesson Five should already be on cards in your Wish Deck. Now I want you to think about the rest of the cards in your Wish Deck the same way: select your favorites and one at a time, imagine you've taken every activity all the way to the top.

You don't have to do any writing for this exercise, *just pay careful attention to your feelings.* If you feel some excitement or happiness when you look at a card, take a moment to picture yourself being in that career. If your card says "pilot," imagine you're at the pinnacle of that career—by your definition. Would you be in your own plane, soaring over the Andes? Or in the cockpit of the Concord on your way to Paris? Doing stunts in an air show or trying out the latest military jet?

If your card says, "politics," imagine yourself winning a local election with all your helpers cheering, or standing up in Congress fighting for a bill you believe in, or visiting a foreign country on a fact-finding mission: whatever would be the height of that career for you.

Look at every card. Don't concern yourself with what your family or friends would think; ask yourself only what *you* would see as the pinnacle of that career. Imagine it for a moment. Pay close attention to your feelings, and if you find that fantasy enjoyable, place that card on the right side of the table. You'll be using it in just a moment.

If a card doesn't wake up a warm feeling of pleasure, place it to your left. When you've finished this step, wrap these cards in a rubber band and put them aside. You won't be using them for now. *But don't throw them away.* Something made you consider those ideas long enough to include them, and you should definitely go through them again sometime to see if they will speak more clearly to you.

For now, all we're concerned with are the cards on the table to your right.

Step 2: Repeat the fantasy for two minutes

Back in Step 1 you took a brief moment to picture yourself doing every activity you wrote on a card. Now, with the remaining cards, repeat this step, but this time take at least two full minutes for each fantasy. *This won't be easy.* Two minutes is longer than you think, and fantasizing can be hard. Here's how to do it.

If your first card says, "Olympic swimmer," close your eyes and pretend you're swimming in the Olympics. Feel the water rushing by you, notice the sound in your ears, feel your arms stretching out, your muscles pulling you ahead. Sense the intensity of the moment, the audience, the television cameras up in the stands. Above all, give the fantasy time to grow. After you've imagined swimming a full lap or two, imagine you're pulling yourself out of the water and standing beside the pool with a towel over your shoulders. Look around you at the admiring audience, at the coach. Make the fantasy as real as you possibly can.

Then open your eyes, pick up your pencil and move right to Step 3.

Step 3: What was the best part of each fantasy?

For example, if you picked "Olympic swimmer," what was the best part for you? The drive to win? The cheer of the crowd? Your arms pulling you through the water? Think carefully. As soon as you have the answer (or answers) draw a small heart on the left side of the card, directly under the title, and write your answer next to it. Hearts are a little sappy, but they will remind you at a glance that you're talking about *feelings,* not reason. Only feelings will tell you what you need to know in this exercise.

On Jay's card, "Travel," he wrote that he loved best "meeting gentle people different from my own, the free time and open spaces, experiencing new sounds and smells."

Bennett's card also said "Travel," but she loved best "learning about new cultures, getting away from home."

And Alicia, still another travel lover, said her favorite part of traveling was having so many "Sights, pictures, colors to photograph. And having so many exciting stories to bring back."

All of us love something special about any activity. We rarely have a chance to examine what it is, however, and we almost never explain it to each other. Our experiences are so unique that it's hard to find the words to explain why they're delightful to us. We usually give up and say, "There's no accounting for taste."

As a result, we either feel isolated and different, or we assume that everyone loves what we love for the same reason so there's nothing special about us at all.

But you *are* special. And when you find your gifts you'll never feel isolated again. Why? For one, your work itself will become a wonderful companion for you. Not only that, when you start to show your talent, and people start to see the results, they'll begin to understand and even encourage you. And when you finally become an expert—which is what usually happens when you follow your gifts—they'll soon come asking for advice.

But until that time, you're on your own. *Finding your path belongs only to you.* No one else knows where you're supposed to go because they can't understand what you feel. But with every response you have to each fantasy, you will fill in another part to the puzzle of who you are and what you should be doing.

When you're finished writing about what you loved best and

> *Travel*
> ♥ *Meeting gentle people different
> from my own, the free time
> and open spaces, experiencing new
> sounds and smells.*

putting a heart next to it on the first card, return to the Wish Deck and repeat Step 2 and 3 for each of the remaining cards. Take the time to fantasize every activity in great detail. Wake up your senses and your feelings so you can figure out what you loved best about it.

Seek similarities: themes from the Wish Deck

When you've gone through every card, take a look at your answers to the question of what was the best part of the fantasy for you. Do you see any themes or patterns occurring? Are you finding that you love to perform, or to compete and win, or to be creative in your own business, or work with colors, or use your physical strength, or work by yourself, or work in a team? Underline the thoughts that keep showing up.

What about the contradictions?

Jay, who loved travel, noticed that many of his other cards showed a love of being at home. What does this mean? Well, it means something different to everyone. Jay figured out that he loved working at home but needed to refresh himself by traveling to his favorite places at least twice a year. "I thought I loved travel for itself, but I think I really only like to go to Spain, to my favorite seaside town. I love it there. And then I like to come home to my nest."

Now, open your notebook to a new sheet of paper, put the date in the upper right hand corner, head it "Themes from the Wish Deck," and write down everything these exercises reveal. Don't stop until you've written down absolutely everything you're learning, everything that's coming into your mind as a result of this step. Take as much time as you need. Fill up as many pages as you can, without editing. Write until you run dry.

Then put the notebook down and take a break of at least a few hours. When you return, take your pen and draw a box around any words or sentences that look especially interesting or important to you.

Don't look now but the outline of your special gift is starting to appear.

Step 4: Cut the deck

If you found that you have a strong love for being outdoors, or for working with ideas, or for looking at things that are visually exciting—or all three, and all of them seem very important to you—place the cards on which you've signaled out these qualities to the right as you go through the deck. Any cards that have no significant theme and aren't essential to you, place to your left with the other cards you discarded.

Here's what Vincent discovered:

Vincent: "The most important theme that kept showing up was a desire to do some good in this world, something important. To me, that meant making a difference to people, turning someone's life around. Another theme was important, too, and that was a desire to be respected for the good I do. Most of the other cards showed that I love to go hiking and play tennis, and I love going to the movies, but I'd be satisfied to do those on the side."

Do the same with your deck. Whittle it down to the most important cards.

In the next step you're going to put even more time and effort into examining the remaining cards so remove all but the most important ones from the deck.

Step 5: Pros and Cons

In your notebook, at the top of a fresh sheet of paper, write the heading from the first card in your deck. Let's say it says "Work with porpoises." Now draw a line down the middle of the page, making two columns. Over the right column write "Good idea because . . ." and over the left column write "Big problem be-cause . . ."

If you're like the woman in Lesson Nine who worked in an office "pushing papers," in the "Good idea" column you might write "it's healthier than what I do now," "I'd be so good at it," "worthwhile," while in the left column, under "Big problem," you might write "I live far from the sea," or "who would hire a begin-ner like me?"

Got it? All right, now using a different sheet of paper for each card, go through every remaining one in your deck and write down why each activity is a good idea and what the big problem is. (Remember the very first suggestion in the Idea Bank in Lesson Seven? It was called "the wish/obstacle solution." This is the same idea. So, take your time and frame the good reasons and the prob-lems as specifically as you can.

Big problem because...
I live far from the sea.
Who would hire a beginner like me?

Work With Porpoises

Good idea because...
It's healthier than what I do now.
I'd be so good at it.
Worthwhile

Step 6: Find some solutions

Everything you wrote in the left-hand columns of each page is a problem waiting for a solution. This is the time for an Idea Party, or a visit to the library, or the Internet. Somewhere out there I can promise you someone has a very good idea for you.

But first, take a look at every sheet. Is it worth this investment in time and effort? The only way to know is to see how you feel about what is written there. If you're not curious enough to do some more investigating, discard the sheet and the card it was taken from. But if those activities still exert a pull on your heart, go and find out more about them. All of them.

Don't look now but you're turning into an expert

When you're finished with these steps you'll be an insider in everything you investigated. You'll know so much about working with dolphins, or careers in travel, or becoming a speaker on the lecture circuit that you'll wonder why you ever thought it was impossible. Even if you haven't decided to act on this particular wish, you're going to change from a person who thinks that dreams are only dreams into a person who knows that it's possible to turn any dream into a reality. That's a huge transformation.

None of this learning will be wasted. Everything you find will be useful to you because you're searching in the right general area. If desire led you to this area, you're hot on the trail of work that's right for you.

And if your information makes you decide *against* working with dolphins, traveling, or being a speaker, by the time you're finished overcoming the obstacles, you'll still have found a dozen other ways to use your talents—ways you'd never have known about otherwise. As you saw in the stories in Lesson Nine, becoming knowledgeable and talking to people who are already involved is how amazing lives get built.

After you've done one or two pages and seen how much more possible everything is than you ever imagined, you might decide to jump right over the rest of your Wish Deck and head straight for your "heart-stopper" card. If so, go for it. Skip ahead to Step 7.

But something else might even happen: a long-forgotten dream might suddenly pop into your memory. Dreams aren't so easy to get rid of. They don't go away, they just hide in the back of your mind waiting to see if you'll ever become clever and capable and courageous enough to take proper care of them. They often surface at this time, as shiny and beautiful as when they hid themselves away long ago. If this happens to you, write up a brand new card and put it through all the exercises you've done so far. You may have found your path.

Now there are only two things left to do.

Step 7: Sleep on it

Whether you've chosen the one dream you want to go after, or you're still deciding between several of them, you need some input from your subconscious. This is what your imaginary allies are good at. Right before you go to sleep read through all the remaining cards in your Wish Deck. If you've made a tentative choice, close your eyes and imagine going after it. You want those wishes on your mind as you go to sleep.

Just before you fall asleep, ask your allies a question: "Which one of these dreams is right for me?" or "Have I chosen the best one?" or "Do I have what it takes to follow this dream?" or any other question you choose. Keep paper and pen or a tape recorder by your bedside so you can record any thoughts that come to you in the night or first thing in the morning. Set your alarm to go off early so you can go back to sleep in the morning and give your subconscious thoughts more opportunity to work their magic.

Then turn out the light and go to sleep.

Some people will get the answer handed to them in the morning like a birthday present: "Photography is what you love. Do it," or "You've got what it takes to be a fine painter. And that's what will really make you happy."

Most of us won't be so lucky, but we might get some kind of important information to help us. Whatever comes to mind about your wishes, write it down before you get out of bed, and let yourself continue to think about it during the day.

No matter what outcome the morning brings, the next step is the same.

Step 8: Go to a meeting

Go to the *Encyclopedia of Associations* or look at a trade magazine in the library and find an organization that shares the interest you've chosen. If you haven't made that choice, do this step for every card that remains: call the office, get on the mailing list and attend the next meeting. Take your notebook with you to the meeting, and write down everything of importance that comes your way, in no particular order. Take names, write your thoughts and impressions, describe the people who spoke to the group and why you'd like to talk to them. Pick up announcements and advertisements and tuck them into your notebook. Speak to as many people as you can about what they're doing. And mention your good idea and your big problems (or your wish/obstacle) as often as possible.

Nothing will make this fantasy more real to you than being surrounded by a gathering of people who are involved in it. Even if you speak to no one, standing in a roomful of writers, speakers, or dolphin lovers will make your dream more real than anything else you can do. There they are, people living their life in a way you thought was only a dream. You can't think your dream is unrealistic or impossible after that.

There's sure to be at least one speaker in your area and lots of sheets of information. Whether your obstacle gets solved or not, you're certain to walk out wiser than before.

These eight steps are a major project, but this is your life and the stakes are high. Remember, *you don't have to put your whole life on hold to do them.* You should be going to work as usual, fulfilling your obligations and taking some time to enjoy yourself. That way you won't feel pressured to come up with an answer in a hurry. You're in a process that's a lot like having a baby, so take your time.

When you've completed all eight steps, if you find that you haven't already chosen a goal, you will find that you are within inches of choosing one. And then it will be time to deliver.

Step 9: Pick a goal and get started within three days

Whoops! Do I really mean that? What if you simply can't decide which goal is right for you yet?

Pick one anyway and start going after it

Write the starting date in your calendar and make it three days from this very moment. Why three days? Because you need two days to be scared and rebellious.

Be as negative as you like, wear a sign on your T-shirt that says "We who are about to die, salute you," or "This is the dumbest idea I've ever heard of." Complain to all your friends. Write down every negative feeling you're having. Look at your calendar and your apartment and as you're complaining start clearing some time and space for the project. Enjoy your negativity! Nature put it there to help you release tension, so don't hesitate to use it.

But on the third day get rolling.

Don't empty out your bank account and quit your job just yet, but do begin to take the small steps that will lead you to the dream you've chosen. You can't really go wrong. Every card that's still in your Wish Deck is close enough to lead you to the right goal. And waiting until you get it just right is not a good idea. You've put in a lot of time already and done some superb thinking about what you love. More won't help. Only action will give you any new information.

State your commitment and write your to-do list, or run your wish through outcome thinking, as you did with your press releases. Figure out the first steps you have to take, and attach some tentative dates to them. Call a meeting of your Success Team, gather your imaginary allies and carry your Memory Deck everywhere with you. Everything important that you learned is in that deck, so thumb through it at every opportunity.

You can't get any more ready, and inside you know it. If you're scared, congratulations. That's an almost sure sign that you picked something that matters to you more than anything in the world. If you're having a hard time swinging into action, your resistance is up to its old tricks. It's probably telling you that this is your final decision, so you've got to get it right, or something terrible is going to happen. But resistance is primitive—and it's wrong. Nothing bad is going to happen.

You're just starting to do something very, very new. You're starting to build your life around what you love and nothing will ever be the same.

Is this the final answer for sure? It could be. But if it's not, you'll have all the chances you'll ever need to get it right. Happy people have invariably made many turns and revisions on their way to good lives, and they expect to make more after they've arrived.

They understand that the good life is never actually completed.

They understand something else you may not know: ready or not, the moment you choose an appealing goal and go after it, the good life has already begun.

Epilogue

"Let yourself be silently drawn by the strange pull of what you really love. It will not lead you astray."

R U M I

Dear Barbara,

For so many years, ever since physical problems made me give up singing, I've been keeping away from the music world. A long time ago I told you I could hardly go to an opera because I was so critical of how people were singing. You told me that meant I cared a lot about music and maybe I should teach. I thought I would hate teaching and it would only make me more critical so I didn't agree with you. Well, I finally gave in a few months ago and started taking some singing students. And I'm so surprised I had to write you.

I've been coaching one man and I like it better than I ever thought was possible. When the music on the page comes alive through someone's voice it's incredibly exciting. Watching someone begin to really understand that there is something to the music besides notes and words is thrilling. It changes their whole way of thinking about who they are in music and just what they want to give to the world.

I should have known I could never walk away from music. But I had no idea I'd love teaching so much, that it would make me feel this good.

Thank you.

Love,
Joyce

I know Joyce personally, but all you have to do is read her letter to know how good she is. Look what her student is learning: "there is something to the music besides notes and words . . . It changes their whole way of thinking about who they are in music and just what they want to give to the world."

Joyce is thrilled and her student is having a revelation. That makes her a brilliant teacher, in anybody's terms. And she's obviously living a life she loves.

Now that you've completed all these lessons, you're on your way to a life you will love, too. There's no mistaking it. Everything has changed already. You're definitely not bored anymore, that's for certain. You may already be signed up to take classes in a school you've never been to before. Or be learning to fly a plane, or making maps on a computer, or packing your suitcase to leave for a country you've never seen. You're already meeting new people and learning things you never knew—and feeling a range of emotions you never felt.

You're on your way.

You might also be scared. Your old life may not have been exciting but it was familiar. This path you're on can take your breath away. But remember what you learned. If you're scared, slow down for a moment. There's no need to push yourself. Life is not combat and you're not a soldier (unless of course, you wrote that on your list of favorite motivational methods back in Lesson One.)

What you are is a human being, sensitive and alive, with genius inside of you. Not only that, you're one of a kind. There has never been anyone like you before. You see the world in a unique way because you have unique gifts. That's the way nature made you. And it will feel like nothing less than fulfilling your destiny to follow those gifts to a rich and exciting life, full of purpose and meaning and enjoyment.

You're going to help other people, too. Not only will you be contributing your talent to the world, but the people around you will see how you live and will be inspired to try for a life they love, too.

And you won't feel alone. You've learned to work with your allies and you're on your way to making new friends. Maybe you'll even have a Success Team to support you and cheer you on. But most of all, you've got the incredible companionship of your own gifts, shining out and lighting the path ahead of you. See what's beyond? Work you're going to love.

That love will pull you.

So let me congratulate you. You should be proud of yourself. You've worked hard in these ten lessons and you're well on your way to the payoff. Let yourself enjoy the path you're on and look forward to the life you're creating. You're going to love it.

Benjamin Disraeli said, "Most people go to their graves with their music still in them." I can't think of anything sadder than that. But that doesn't have to happen to you because now you know how to find your music and let it out. You're going to sing a song no one has ever heard before and the world will be more beautiful for it.

I can't wait to hear it—and I thank you in advance.

LIVE
THE
LIFE
YOU
LOVE

TWELVE LESSONS,
ON TWELVE AUDIO CASSETTES

Now that you've read the book, take the next step. In her audio tape program, Barbara will be your personal coach, leading you, step-by-step, through additional lessons unique to this audio tape program. This is not a book on tape. With her warm caring voice, Barbara will help you find your dreams and teach you how to build a life around them. You'll feel like she's in the room with you, offering help and encouragement just when you need it most.

By now you know that everyone has unique gifts and talents, and to be truly happy—to live a completely fulfilled life—you don't have to change yourself, and you don't have to walk out on your responsibilities. You just need to use the gifts that are waiting inside you. You can have a life you love; let Barbara show you how.

TAPE 1 - WHY YOU MUST BE ALL YOU CAN BE
TAPE 2 - MORNING AND EVENING, FIVE MINUTES A DAY
TAPE 3 - A SURPRISING JOURNEY
TAPE 4 - GETTING UNSTUCK
TAPE 5 - RESISTANCE
TAPE 6 - MOVING AND SHAKING
TAPE 7 - SO HOW ARE YOU FEELING NOW?
TAPE 8 - THE IDEA BANK
TAPE 9 - IF I COULD NOT FAIL
TAPE 10 - REAL STORIES
TAPE 11 - HOW TO WRITE YOUR OWN SUCCESS STORY
TAPE 12 - LIVING THE GOOD LIFE

TO ORDER, OR FOR MORE INFORMATION, PLEASE CALL:
1 (800) 548-3027